CW01149306

LESSONS FROM THE ARENA OF RESILIENCE

THE MILES WE RUN

ALISON BEDER SOLWAY

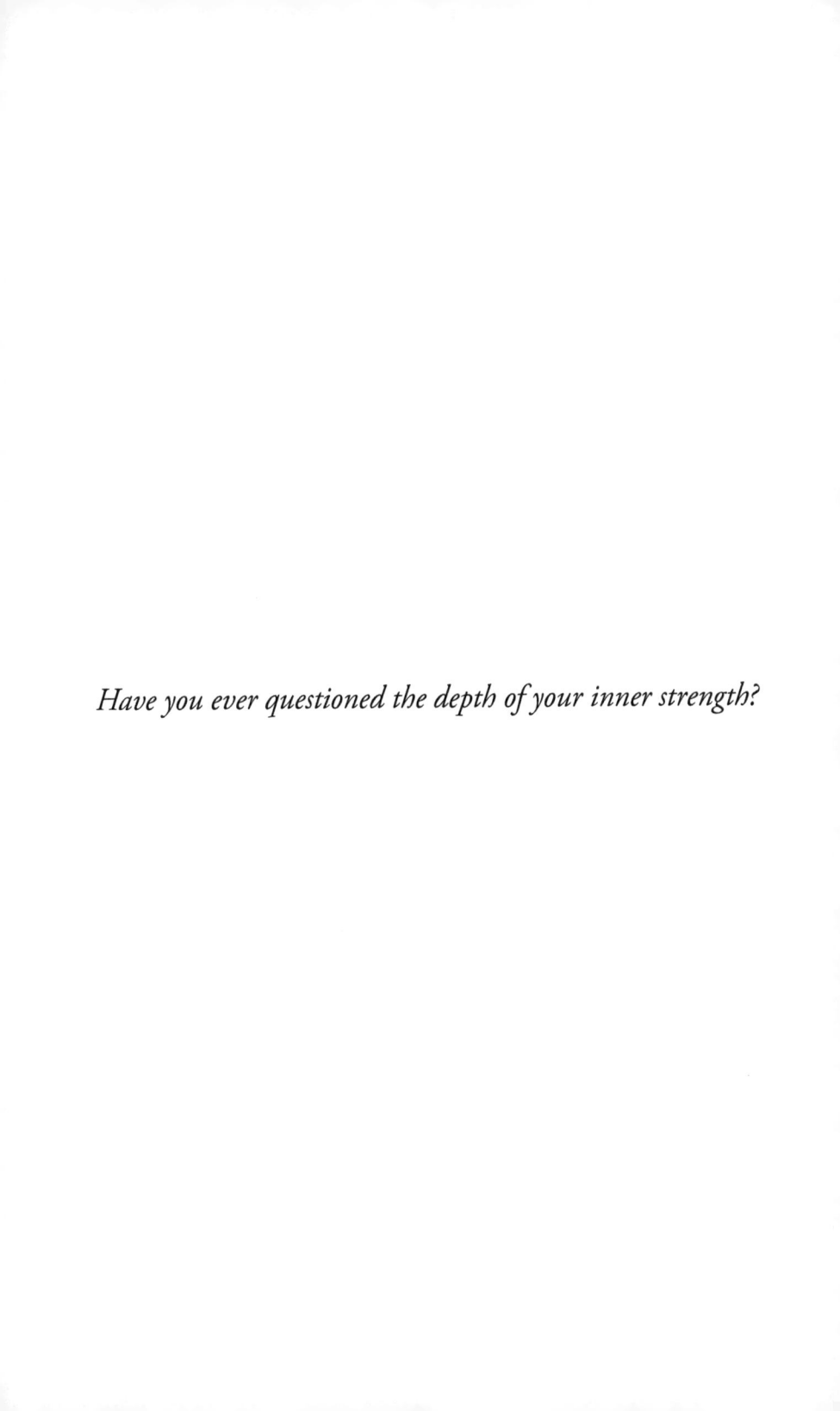

Have you ever questioned the depth of your inner strength?

The Miles We Run
Copyright © 2024 by Alison Beder Solway

All rights reserved. No part of this publication may be reproduced, distributed, or transmitted in any form or by any means, including photocopying, recording, or other electronic or mechanical methods, without the prior written permission of the author, except in the case of brief quotations embodied in critical reviews and certain other non-commercial uses permitted by copyright law.

Author's Note: In crafting the narrative of my memoir, I changed certain names to respect privacy and confidentiality. It's important to understand that my recounting is deeply personal and subjective. It reflects my own experiences, perceptions, and memories. This account is not a substitute for professional, medical, or legal advice.

I hope that by sharing my life's moments they might resonate with, inspire, and offer solace to others navigating their own paths. Through these pages, I invite you into my world. It's as I remember it, shaped by both its imperfections and its beauty.

Cover Design: Alison Beder Solway and Jordan Lunn
Images: Jason Yoder and Mykola Mazuryk; Shutterstock.com
Author Photo: Daniel Kelly

tellwell
Tellwell Talent
www.tellwell.ca

ISBN
978-1-998454-22-8 (Hardcover)
978-1-998454-21-1 (Paperback)
978-1-998454-23-5 (eBook)

H.A.R.C.
I love you. xo.

PRAISE FOR
THE MILES WE RUN

"This book is indispensable. I cannot wait to share it with clients who are undergoing their own surrogacy journey. I love how you share your personal experiences while engaging the reader in reflective questions to dig deeper. This book offers hope and opened my perspective and heart ♥."
— **Amira Posner**, BSW, MSW, registered social worker, and dedicated therapist with extensive experience in supporting individuals and couples facing infertility challenges

"*In The Miles We Run*, Alison has written a rich, poignant, and easy-to-read book. Mile by mile, using the analogy of a marathon, Alison shares her personal story of navigating the deeply complex worlds of high-risk pregnancy, parenting, fertility struggles, and surrogacy, and the immense challenges of these experiences. As a women's mental health psychiatrist, I have seen so many women who have had to face an often challenging healthcare system and overcome Herculean obstacles to build a family. I know people will find comfort in reading Alison's story, they will be inspired by her perseverance and resilience as they are called to reflect on their own path by the author's thoughtful prompts."
— **Ariel Dalfen**, MD, FRCPC, CEO BRIA

"As a fertility lawyer in Canada, I read Alison's book with great curiosity. Alison breathes life into what most only know about, if at all, through the skewed eyes of the media. Her story is filled with determination, compassion, courage, and thoughtful insight into the complicated, overwhelming, and emotional world of surrogacy through the eyes of an intended parent. Alison's bravery is inspiring, her journey is compelling, and her compassion for those who helped her is heartfelt. Thank you for writing this, Alison."

— **Shirley Eve Levitan**, Family and Fertility Law, Canada

"*The Miles We Run* reveals raw personal insights about surrogacy. Alison Beder Solway offers herself as a guide to patients in trusting their instincts and self-advocating in the face of tremendous social and institutional pressure. She ultimately finds her way to self-acceptance in her most vulnerable moments and self-belief in times of despair."

— **Julie Devaney**, health advocate and consultant, author of *My Leaky Body: Tales from the Gurney* and co-editor of *Mess: The Hospital Anthology*

"I loved every word of this inspiring and heartwarming memoir that offers a raw and vulnerable window into the challenging world of surrogacy."

— **Ellen Schwartz**, elementary school teacher, community leader, public speaker, and author of *Lessons from Jacob: A Disabled Son Teaches His Mother About Courage, Hope and the Joy of Living Each Day to the Fullest* and *Without One Word Spoken*

To every woman daring greatly by being in the arena. May courage be your compass, strength your stride, and joy your light as you navigate the challenges in your own life's marathon.

CONTENTS

Preface 1

PART I

Introduction 5

Mile 1:   My Starting Line 9
Mile 2:   The *Why* 15
Mile 3:   A Love Story 19
Mile 4:   Pregnancy 25
Mile 5:   HHT 37
Mile 6:   Training and Trails 42
Mile 7:   The Road to Surrogacy 46
Mile 8:   Too Good to Be True 52

PART II

Mile 9:   Disillusion and Disappointment 61
Mile 10: Chasing Miracles 70
Mile 11: The Balance of Rhythm 77
Mile 12: Education vs. Persuasion 81
Mile 13: At the Crossroads 96

PART III

Mile 14:	Welcome to the U.S.A.	109
Mile 15:	Timelines and Landmines	118
Mile 16:	On the Cusp	128
Mile 17:	The Surreal Is Real	134
Mile 18:	The Complexity of Creation	145
Mile 19:	Between Two Worlds	152
Mile 20:	A Rebirth	160

PART IV

Mile 21:	Here We Go Again	175
Mile 22:	Two for the Road	184
Mile 23:	Life After Surrogacy	193
Mile 24:	Lessons Learned	206
Mile 25:	Race Day	211
Mile 26.2:	Hope	215
Mile 27:	TBD	217

Acknowledgments 219

PREFACE

It's intriguing to realize that you're closer to the conclusion of your own life than to its commencement. At fifty-three, I've quite probably lived more than half of my existence. Of course, I write this without the prescience of what tomorrow may bring. I often contemplate the myriad experiences that have led me to this juncture, wondering, *Could others derive value and inspiration from what has shaped my identity?*

As you read *The Miles We Run* and engage with the struggles, triumphs, and revelations that have influenced me, I invite you to delve into your own life. Let my stories within these pages spark introspection and newfound awareness in you. The true essence of this memoir lies not just in the narratives I share but in the questions and insights they may awaken within you. Embrace these moments of reflection as stepping stones on your own unique path, revealing the profound hope and resilience in your personal story.

PART I

"It is not the critic who counts; not the woman who points out how the strong woman stumbles, or where the doer of deeds could have done them better. The credit belongs to the woman who is actually in the arena, whose face is marred by dust and sweat and blood; who strives valiantly; who errs, who comes short again and again, because there is no effort without error and shortcoming; but who does actually strive to do the deeds; who knows great enthusiasms, the great devotions; who spends herself in a worthy cause; who at the best knows in the end the triumph of high achievement, and who at the worst, if she fails, at least fails while daring greatly, so that her place shall never be with those cold and timid souls who neither know victory nor defeat." —Theodore Roosevelt[1]

---

[1] "The Man in the Arena" is an excerpt from Theodore Roosevelt's "Citizenship in a Republic" speech given at the Sorbonne in Paris, France, on April 23, 1910. I have adapted the text to reflect "the man" in the arena as a woman.

INTRODUCTION

In the arena of life, I stand resolute, my journey evident in the dust, sweat, and tears that have graced my face. With steadfast courage, I've taken risks, stared down challenges, and dared to dream audaciously. Yet I've also stumbled, felt the sting of defeat, and been humbled by setbacks. Time and again, these experiences have instilled in me a great understanding: from the moment we take our first breath, the clock starts ticking toward our inevitable end. But rather than a somber realization, it's a call to action. The canvas between our birth and death is vast, and the beauty lies not in the certainty of its completion but in the vibrant, unpredictable, and meaningful panorama we create along the way.

When I was ten years old and my brother, Adam, was eight, my sister came into the world. Aarin's birth marked a turning point for me. The first time I held her, I was overwhelmed by a deep yearning to become a mother someday. As time passed and I watched Aarin grow from a baby into a toddler, my vision for my future family became even more vivid. I pictured maybe three kids—a dynamic akin to my life with two siblings. I imagined a household buzzing with energy, the floor a mosaic of Legos and tiny shoes, and a home filled with laughter and joy. Above all, I saw myself holding a baby, feeling that inexplicable love, aware that this newborn human was intrinsically connected to me. Little did I realize that my aspiration to become a mother would not only push the boundaries of my resilience but also lead me through a near-death experience and a surrogacy odyssey that would span more than four years.

My father's passion for running significantly influenced my siblings and me. Whether through genetic predisposition or inspired by his example, we have all adopted this pursuit with equal fervor. Even at eighty-five years old, he continues to lace up his running shoes and hit the pavement, albeit not at the same pace he maintained two decades ago. The important thing is that he's still running, demonstrating a remarkable dedication to the sport that has left a lasting impact on all of us.

During the two years of the COVID-19 crisis, Adam, Aarin, and I ran together every Saturday morning, covering a distance of 6.2 miles (10 kilometers/km). It became a weekly ritual for us to spend time together in a safe space, engaging in an activity we all loved. It's a tradition we continue to this day.

I knew that if I were to run a marathon, undeniably it would be the iconic New York City (NYC) Marathon. Initially, I aimed to participate at the age of fifty, but the pandemic caused me to postpone this goal until I was fifty-one. Once I'd registered, I was excited to share my news. When I phoned my brother, there was an audible gasp on the other end: he had signed up just a week earlier. Riding on this wave of coincidence, I called Aarin, who exclaimed without hesitation, "Well, if you two are doing it, so am I!"

For me, it was a formidable challenge upon reaching my half-century mark. I yearned to embark on a personal quest where I could step outside my comfort zone and demonstrate to myself that I could still do hard things.

Introduction

As I steer through the second act of my life, where introspection guides my intentions, words, and actions, I realized that running the NYC Marathon was about much more than physical endurance. It symbolized distinct chapters of my life—family, ambition, struggle, and resilience—and served as a powerful metaphor for life itself. When I crossed the finish line on that humid November afternoon in New York City, after running for 4 hours, 54 minutes, and 6 seconds, a cascade of emotions washed over me: joy, exhilaration, validation, love, support, discomfort, pain, and vulnerability.

This memoir charts the intimate journey of my four-year surrogacy experience some two decades prior, revealing layers of resilience I hadn't known I possessed, which were later mirrored in the stamina required for my marathon training. It is a story woven with enduring optimism and strength. It is a tale of triumph against the odds, told to kindle hope and to confirm that the goals we strive to achieve are attainable when we commit to persist.

I invite you to journey through *The Miles We Run* with me, to navigate the challenges and embrace the victories. Within my story, I hope you find a source of inspiration, confirming that in life's rigorous race, every step taken, even in doubt, can propel us toward a magnificent culmination.

Dearest Reader: Have you pursued a goal that pushed you beyond your comfort zone? How did it affect you?

MILE 1

MY STARTING LINE

The familiar notes of Frank Sinatra's "New York, New York" filled the air. As the anticipation built, thousands of runners stood poised at the starting line: excited, anxious, hopeful, and, above all, focused. After nine months of training, I was awestruck that I had made it there. I was keenly aware that everyone in this corral was set to embark upon their own unique path—it wasn't about outdoing anyone else. The preparation, though critically important, suddenly seemed trivial. The real challenge would be in summoning the psychological strength to negotiate the upcoming 26.2 miles (42.2 km). One step at a time would become one mile, then two, and that was to be my approach. When the U.S. national anthem started to play, a calm determination settled over me. As the gun sounded, it became clear that this was my moment to affirm my potential—not to anyone else but to myself.

The race begins with the Verrazzano Bridge, presenting runners with a steady incline for nearly a mile. It's an uphill battle right from the beginning. The irony is that the adrenaline from the excitement of the race makes the challenge almost imperceptible. However, if you push yourself too hard at this early stage—a common mistake for many runners, especially first-time marathoners like myself—you are likely to face uncomfortable consequences later in the race.

Similar to this first demanding mile, life does not afford everyone the privilege of a level start. I am lucky to have entered the world with various advantages, growing up in the vibrant and diverse city of Toronto, Canada. My upbringing was characterized by a cozy home life, parents who provided love, support, and a degree of stability that isn't a universal experience. While the full scope of my privilege wasn't entirely clear to me in my younger years, my parents, Robert and Sharron, made sure to emphasize the importance of humility in our household. These essential teachings were shared with me and my siblings, shaping a foundational ethos that has accompanied us throughout our lives.

Participating in a marathon is a grounding ordeal. You might enter the race feeling fully ready and self-assured, but the actual event is fraught with uncertainties. Every beginning brims with boundless potential, but our paths often narrow as we move farther from the start. *Isn't this a reflection of life itself?* We pour our energy into goals, only to meet unexpected challenges or unplanned diversions that compel us to shift directions.

At thirteen years old, my understanding of the privileges I'd been afforded was magnified in a defining moment during a family getaway. A persistent, piercing pain in my right leg had been bothering me throughout the trip, becoming especially unbearable at night. Back in Toronto, my mother promptly took me to our family doctor for an X-ray. As we awaited the results, I tried to distract myself by attending a movie with a friend. There I was, sitting in a theater captivated by Matt Dillon in *The Flamingo Kid*. Just as I thought I'd found a brief escape from the constant pain, a spotlight from an usher interrupted the movie. Behind him was my teary-eyed mother, informing me that we had to leave immediately. The results of the X-ray were in, and they couldn't wait.

After making sure my friend would be picked up by her mother, we rushed to Toronto's Sick Kids Hospital, where my dad was waiting for us. An empathetic pediatric orthopedic surgeon outlined the worrisome findings on my right femur bone. The plain white walls of the hospital room seemed to close in on me. The doctor's words—"possible cancer, surgery needed"—echoed in my head, each syllable a heavy drumbeat against my youthful innocence. In those moments, the world shifted; the games, the schoolyard laughs, all faded into the background. I remember staring at my small, shaking hands, twisting a gold ring around my finger, a stark contrast to the enormity of what I was facing. It was as if I could see the threads of my once predictable life unraveling, each one a reminder of how quickly everything could change. That day, for the first time, I faced my mortality. Confronting such dire possibilities made me realize how fragile the balance of life is, and it shook the foundation of my previously sheltered existence.

My parents were visibly distraught—a sight that was both unfamiliar and disconcerting. Their expressions, always warm and reassuring, now reflected the seriousness of the situation. Despite doing everything they could to soothe me with comforting words and gentle hugs, a pervasive fear took hold of me. In the midst of this anxiety, however, there was a faint but steady voice within. At that time, it didn't articulate my now-familiar adage of *you can do hard things*. It was more like a quiet hum, a subtle undercurrent of resilience that I didn't fully understand but intuitively clung to. It was this unspoken assurance, more felt than heard, that helped me to bear the weight of the uncertainty and fear.

The surgery was performed successfully two days later. The weight lifted as we received the news that it wasn't cancer but rather osteomyelitis,[1] an infection that had spread along the femur bone in my right leg.

Due to the severity of the infection, the medical team had to meticulously scrape away the affected bone tissue. This intensive procedure left me with a long road to recovery. I was facing a three-month rehabilitation to regain strength and functionality in my leg, commencing while I was still in the hospital.

The healing process was both a physical and mental ordeal. Each small improvement, no matter how trivial it seemed, was a victory in my eyes as I regained autonomy over my body. I remember how my physiotherapist suggested using my dad's stationary bicycle as part of my rehabilitation. The guidance was precise: pedal gently just a quarter stroke with my right leg, then slowly bring the pedal back with the help of my left. This wasn't just a strategic exercise designed to restore range of motion; it was an invaluable lesson in patience.

Despite the clear instructions, my stubborn desire to accelerate my recovery tempted me to push beyond the boundaries set by my physiotherapist. Driven by curiosity and a youthful sense of invulnerability, I decided to extend past the prescribed quarter stroke. The consequence was immediate

---

[1] Osteomyelitis is a bone infection commonly caused by bacteria, arising from direct contamination, bloodstream spread, or neighboring infections. Symptoms include pain, fever, and swelling at the infection site. Treatment often involves antibiotics and possibly surgery. Sources: Based on data up to September 2021 from the Centers for Disease Control and Prevention, World Health Organization, and Mayo Clinic.

and jarring—a sharp scream reverberated throughout our house as a searing pain radiated down my leg, igniting the fear of causing permanent damage.

In a panic, my mom phoned the doctor. While the pain gradually subsided, the uncertainty lingered until the doctor's words offered a new perspective: "Slow and steady wins the race." At thirteen, grappling with such a daunting task, this phrase shifted from a mere cliché to a guiding principle. It emerged as a revelation, shedding light on my path to recovery with newfound clarity and purpose.

Embracing the *slow and steady wins the race* mantra, I approached the pedal exercises with a renewed sense of commitment and patience. I experienced how discipline impacts both the physical and mental realms, and how perseverance and endurance foster well-being in both body and mind. It laid a foundational mindset for my future, anchoring the insights gained during recovery. This realization resurfaced later in my passion for running: recognizing the importance of steady progress, the strength in persistence, and the wisdom in valuing the process over the outcome.

During my hospital stay, the overwhelming support from family, friends, and well-wishers provided me with another fundamental insight. Balloons, flowers, and tokens of encouragement filled my room, reminding me of the love and care in my life. I couldn't help but notice the contrast between my experience and that of some other children on my floor. While my space was adorned with gifts, their tables and shelves were bare. The guilt and gratitude intertwined within me, urging me to appreciate the abundance I had been blessed with and to extend kindness to others. Motivated to bring color and joy to the other children's rooms, I gladly distributed my balloons, flowers, and sweet treats. This simple act of sharing, and witnessing the happiness it brought, instilled in me a profound sense of fulfillment.

I left the hospital with a tangible memento of my ordeal: a linear scar running the length of my thigh. Yet, this scar transcended the physical; it became an emblem of fortitude, fragility, and tenacity. It is the symbol of a significant struggle I triumphed over.

Although I may not have had complete comprehension of my privileged background in my youthful years, the insight I gained from that hospital experience has become an inseparable part of my identity today. It has been instrumental in helping me understand, acknowledge, and value the advantages life has bestowed upon me.

For the marathon, my preparation and resilience got me to the finish line, but my upbringing and support system made it possible for me to be at the starting line. Similarly, my recovery from osteomyelitis was not just a feat of medical intervention but a testament to the layers of advantage that cushioned my fall: prompt surgical attention, emotional support, and the security of knowing I was not alone. These experiences have taught me that life's marathons can be as humbling as they are empowering, illuminating not just our strengths but also the invisible wind at our back.

Dearest Reader: Amid personal struggles, how often do you pause to consider the privileges you may take for granted? How does this awareness influence your interactions with others, fostering empathy and compassion for those whose journeys have been more arduous?

MILE 2

THE *WHY*

The question *Why me?* is universal, pondered during each twist and turn of life. But only recently have I started applying this question to the blessings, not just the misfortunes.

Why is such a powerful catalyst for insight and understanding. It fuels our curiosity, deepens our understanding, and sharpens our critical thinking, transcending languages and cultures. Consider the countless instances you've found yourself asking a litany of *why* questions: *Why is this happening to me? Why don't they like me? Why did they do that? Why did I do that? Why is this so hard? Why can't I? Why shouldn't I? Why not?* and so on.

This barrage of *why* queries isn't just a string of words but an echo of our most intimate concerns, fears, and curiosities. Each *why* peels back a layer of the proverbial onion, seeking to uncover the core truth of our experiences and interpersonal dynamics. In both our highs and lows, *why* serves as an investigative tool that probes the external world and prompts us to scrutinize our motivations, ethics, and emotional complexities. Whether we're navigating the turbulence of human relationships, braving daunting challenges, or celebrating unexpected blessings, the question

Why? continually nudges us closer to a fuller understanding and a more intense sense of gratitude and self-awareness.

The question *Why am I running a marathon?* reverberated through my rigorous training and the event itself, mirroring other existential *why* questions. As the physical and mental demands escalated, the question transformed into a meditative maxim, guiding each step and mile. At first, I sought a clear, definitive answer—some singular insight to justify the pain, sweat, and fatigue. But as the miles piled up, it dawned on me: the *why* wasn't tied to a single revelatory moment; it was being shaped by the journey itself.

On one of my longer training runs in Northern Ontario, I remember pausing atop a hill—not in search of breath, but in awe of the vast landscape before me, of being a part of something greater. I realized then how incredible it was that my legs, my lungs, and my heart were all working together to get me to this point. I experienced a genuine thankfulness for what my body could do, a feeling that often gets lost in the shuffle of tracking distances, times, and personal bests. This moment of reflection, surrounded by nature's grandeur, was a powerful reminder of my evolving *why*—not merely a quest for finish lines but an authentic appreciation for the resilience forged along the way.

It's easy to get caught up in chasing goals, so focused on the finish line that we forget to appreciate the run itself. *Have you ever caught yourself missing the view because you were too busy worrying about what's next?* That day was a reminder for me that sometimes the most important part of the journey is recognizing and valuing the effort it takes to simply move forward.

My *why* emerged from a mosaic of experiences like these, each contributing to a nuanced understanding of my own accomplishments, tenacity, and personal growth.

I can't pinpoint the exact moment I decided to run a marathon. Maybe it was the allure of a major physical achievement or the thrill of racing through the streets of New York City. But when I began sharing my goal out loud, the stakes became real—laden with weight and expectation.

During those extended, solitary runs, I honed my skills in self-negotiation. Each outing began with a modest pact: *Let's tackle the first three miles.* As I reached each milestone, I would extend my target—first to five miles, then to seven. Despite having a predetermined distance in mind, these incremental goals served as my psychological safety net, a "just in case" fallback I secretly knew I'd never need.

This internal negotiation became an unspoken guide. As I surpassed the thirteen-mile mark, the physical challenges intensified. Yet, it was the mental struggle, the ongoing inner dialogue, that proved to be the true battleground. Enduring the physical strain was one thing, but mastering the mental challenge, coaxing myself through every stride and breath, was another. This realization was transformative; my *why* transcended the race itself, taking root in the journey that had led me to it.

Just like my training, as I navigated the transitions from adolescence to motherhood, my *why* continued to evolve. It became clear that my purpose extended far beyond the marathon's finish line, indelibly shaped by the entirety of my life's experiences.

Dearest Reader: Reflect on how the question **Why?** *has influenced your journey. How has it shaped your curiosity, understanding, and self-awareness through life's highs and lows?*

MILE 3

A LOVE STORY

Is "love at first sight" real?

Before stepping into Madison Avenue Pub in Toronto, when I was twenty, I had heard tales of this notion but never truly believed it or that it would happen to me. It was a May evening in 1992, a time stamped in my memory, poised to debunk my skepticism in the most enchanting way. The bar was brimming with my peers, mostly university students, and amid laughter and chatter with my friends, my eyes locked onto a man across the room. It wasn't just his appearance but something more profound. I leaned in toward my girlfriend Melissa, pointed to the man, and whispered, "I'm going to marry him." A bold statement, perhaps, but I felt an inexplicable certainty. Saying those words out loud gave them gravity, like a vow uttered before an altar. When my eyes met those of Kenny Solway, there was a jolt of electricity. With his windswept long hair, sun-kissed skin, and eyes that hinted at alluring adventures, he was captivating in a way that left me breathless.

Over the following weeks, fate seemed to conspire to bring us together. We repeatedly crossed paths in the most unexpected places—lively bars, crowded movie theaters, and vibrant dance clubs. I was spellbound by his incredible stories, especially about his solo expedition through Australia and New Zealand. But it was now my time to venture off, and Europe awaited. A summer backpacking trip with my best friend Alana was in the pipeline, requiring me to temporarily freeze whatever was simmering between Kenny and me. My journal from that trip is filled with thoughts of him—beginning, middle, and end. *An ironic foreshadowing? Probably.*

Upon my return to the University of Western Ontario (UWO) in London, Ontario, for my senior year, I harbored hopes of picking up where Kenny and I had left off—except that rumors hinted he was involved with someone else. But life has its own script. During one of his visits to friends at UWO, our paths crossed once again. In that moment, my heart stilled, acknowledging what words couldn't express. Deep down, I knew it wasn't a question of *if* but *when* we would be together. A couple of months later, while I was cleaning up from dinner, the phone rang. It was Kenny. Alana, now my roommate and confidante in all things Kenny, practically pirouetted into the kitchen to tell me. Nerves be damned, this was it.

My first outing with him wasn't just a casual dinner date but a full-blown bash for his birthday and an initiation into his inner circle. He valued this tradition—a relaxed, no-fuss pizza and beer party at his parents' house in Toronto. You know, the kind of event where you really want to look your best, especially since it was taking place in his family home, surrounded by his closest friends and relatives.

Having returned to Toronto for the weekend, I was eagerly anticipating the party. On the morning of the celebration, I decided to get a lip wax—an essential step in taming the enthusiastic overgrowth that my genetics had so generously bestowed upon me. This time, the session took a painful turn; not only did the esthetician remove the unwanted hair, but she also accidentally stripped off a patch of skin from each corner of my mouth. Armed with a face that looked like I'd tried to eat spicy hot wings blindfolded, I faced a dilemma. *To go or not to go?* But backing out was not an option. Instead, I pushed past my self-doubt. *And you know what?* While I might've felt like I was sporting a makeshift clown smile with those two red splotches, leaning into the silliness of the situation turned out to be the best concealer I could have applied. Ultimately, it appeared that no one noticed, or if they did, it simply didn't make a difference.

Kenny and I dated for four years, during which our relationship was put to the test when I relocated to New Hampshire in the U.S., for two years to pursue my Master of Science in environmental studies. Our dedication, however, remained unwavering, even during a time when email was more of a novelty than a necessity. We preserved our connection through handwritten letters and the comforting cadence of regular phone calls. In some ways, this phase of our relationship felt like the middle miles of a marathon. Just as a runner has to dig deep and keep going, often in solitude and under physically taxing conditions, we, too, had to show an enduring commitment to nurture our love. In both scenarios, the connection may not be visible, but it's completely felt.

Nothing could have prepared me for March 1996, however, when the ordinary rhythm of our lives (we were living close to each other once more) took a cinematic twist. Kenny mentioned a seemingly innocuous errand, needing to pick something up from Toronto Pearson International Airport. But from the moment we parked, I realized this was no ordinary task. "Let's go inside," he urged and took me to a check-in counter. An airline representative handed over an envelope with my name on it. Inside were my passport, my birth control pills, two tickets to Providenciales, and a tattered map fragment hinting at the adventure ahead.

Two meticulously packed duffel bags stood ready. Kenny's attention to detail was astonishing—he'd even remembered my specific face soap. As we boarded the plane, a second sealed envelope was waiting for me, revealing yet another map fragment and a tantalizing guide to Turks and Caicos, along with more clues. My heart thrummed in my chest, the dots beginning to connect: *This was a treasure hunt, and the prize? Perhaps an engagement ring.*

Settling into our seats, I attempted to coax details out of Kenny, but he simply ordered us drinks and urged patience with a grin. Left with no choice, I surrendered to the thrill of the unfolding expedition, the expansive sky, his knowing smile, and the whirl of anticipation and wonder.

Upon landing in the sun-drenched paradise, we were approached by a stranger with a third envelope in hand, making me quirk an eyebrow in amusement. *Has Kenny enlisted the entire island for this escapade?* As he drove us to a secluded beach property, Kenny announced with a hint of mischief, "We're camping here tonight." A grocery store stop produced another mysterious envelope; and amid all the clues and excitement, sleep was elusive.

Dawn broke with the sight of a majestic catamaran approaching the beach. As we embarked, the captain handed me another clue-containing envelope and offered us flutes of champagne, heralding the start of our sea odyssey. Kenny had packed me a very skimpy bathing suit. With no alternatives at my disposal, I donned the minimal-coverage bikini and hoped not to startle the marine life below. The world beneath the water's surface was surreal—colorful coral, playful fish, and a dolphin that seemed as intrigued by us as we were by it.

By late afternoon, Kenny had chartered another small boat to take us to Iguana Island, following the trail set by the clues. Each passing second felt monumental. Spotting another envelope half buried in the sand, I pieced together the entire map. As the sun set, painting the sky with vibrant shades of orange, pink, and purple, I was surrounded by unspeakable beauty. Heart pounding, I followed the directions and uncovered a series of intricate little treasure boxes: the smallest among them cradled a dazzling ring. Kenny, eyes sparkling with hope, went down on one knee. The map's inscription read, *I have found great fortune in your beauty and friendship. Please marry me.* Overwhelmed with emotion, tears in my eyes, I whispered, "Yes." We're now approaching twenty-nine years of marriage.

Running has always been an intensely personal space for me, where I can be with my thoughts, goals, and struggles. While I enjoy the camaraderie running alongside my siblings, the experience is largely introspective. In a race surrounded by a sea of competitors, I'm essentially alone with my inner dialogue. Other runners might influence my pace or motivate me, but at the end of the day, it's my own resolve and stamina that carries me to the finish line.

This holds true in relationships as well. Kenny has helped fortify the essence of who I am. He's more than just a partner; he's a vital complement to my individual journey, enriching it and giving it new dimensions without overshadowing my own sense of self.

No matter how our day unfolds, we fall asleep with our fingers intertwined. We often joke about our queen-sized bed—he admittedly wishes we'd opted for a king, whereas I relish the closeness our queen ensures. I wake up feeling lucky. Our journey hasn't been devoid of storms, but even through disagreements and setbacks, our bond has thrived on respect, open dialogue, and an unyielding commitment to find common ground. Every day, I look forward to the miles we have yet to travel together.

Dearest Reader: Can a single moment truly define a connection that lasts a lifetime?

MILE 4

PREGNANCY

Becoming pregnant with Hannah felt like the first exhilarating moments of a sprint—a burst of speed, a gust of wind in my face, an open track ahead. It was joyous, almost effortless, a heart-pounding beginning. No sooner had Kenny and I broached the topic of starting a family than I was staring down at a pregnancy test, mesmerized by those two unmistakable lines. The realization that I was nurturing a new life within me was nothing short of magical.

My foray into motherhood began with the quest for the perfect OB/GYN. In Toronto, one obstetrician was the talk of the town among expectant mothers. Given her sky-high demand, I reasoned she had to be the best. I dialed her office repeatedly, practically groveling to her receptionist for the chance to be taken under this acclaimed physician's wing. At last, my tenacity bore fruit—I snagged an appointment.

As a new mom-to-be, I was stepping into uncharted territory. I had no personal blueprint for how pregnancy would transform my body or a comprehensive grasp of what awaited me. None of my close friends had yet to embark on this path, and my primary point of reference was my mother's pregnancy with Aarin. I vividly recall how she—at age thirty-five, considered advanced for childbirth at that time—gracefully embraced those nine months. Amid this landscape of unknowns, my dedication was clear: I was determined to deliver a healthy, thriving baby into the world.

Throughout the early stages of my pregnancy, I underwent monthly checkups to monitor my vitals and the baby's growth. However, as I progressed deeper into the second trimester, the subtle distress signals from my body became increasingly hard to ignore. I was five months along and already panting like a marathon runner when I walked to the mailbox at the end of our street. My obstetrician was always quick to brush off my concerns. "Shortness of breath is common," she'd say. Yet, the disquiet within me grew; my body seemed to be whispering that all was not well.

Despite the escalating challenges, I treasured every second of my pregnancy, fully conscious of the extraordinary privilege it was to carry a child. Feeling the baby flutter inside me and witnessing my belly dance with their movements were cherished moments. The ultrasound appointments brought Kenny and me immense joy as we listened to the precious heartbeat and witnessed the incredible growth of the baby before our eyes. I couldn't help but marvel at the miracle taking shape within me, remaining grateful no matter the difficulties I faced with my breathing.

By the time I hit the eighth month, simple tasks had morphed into Herculean efforts. My office commute to downtown Toronto, once an easy subway ride, became an ordeal. Either Kenny had to drive me or I braved the traffic myself. Walking felt like wading through quicksand. My body was a sponge, retaining more water than seemed humanly possible. There is typical swelling, and then there was mine: alarmingly pronounced. Frighteningly, my labia now resembled a cow's udder, making me feel as though I was maneuvering a new appendage between my legs. The situation reached such absurdity that I half-expected to start mooing. It was time to step back from work.

April 1, 1999, was no ordinary Thursday. It heralded the Good Friday long weekend and the onset of Passover. As an environmental consultant at an engineering firm, I was involved in creating environmental management plans for companies adapting to new government regulations, and crafting guidelines for corporations to enhance their environmental mindfulness and operational practices. With a hug to my colleagues, I waddled out, leaving my professional realm to embrace an entirely new, deeply personal journey: maternity leave.

The underground parking lot stretched before me like a desert. With each step, my lungs clawed for air. I was almost audibly gasping. Enough was enough. I veered course and steered myself straight to Women's College Hospital (WCH), driven by a pressing need for medical attention.

From the nursing station, I made an urgent call to Kenny. This was before cellphones were an integral part of our daily lives. He sped to the hospital as if every second counted. Tests were conducted, heartbeats monitored—mine was growing increasingly erratic while the baby's remained steady and constant, for which I was profoundly thankful. Doubt swallowed me whole. *Had I betrayed my instincts? Had I been foolish not to question my doctor's complacency?* My usually steely will crumbled, replaced by a dread that clouded my thoughts and made each strained breath a fragile hold on stability. It was as if my body had been screaming, and I had only begun to listen. And as I lay there in the hospital, in a cocoon of worry and anticipation, I knew that what would unfold next was far beyond what any prenatal book had prepared me for.

The moment I was admitted to the high-risk pregnancy ward, a sense of urgency filled the air. Soon after, Dr. Peter Romano, a young and focused OB/GYN, came to see me. As he spoke, the gravity of my situation settled in: I wasn't going home anytime soon. Our baby would likely be born within the next few days. And I was in right congestive heart failure. A shiver ran down my spine. His calm demeanor could not entirely conceal the pressing nature of that diagnosis. He explained that the right side of my heart was struggling to pump blood effectively to my lungs. This was causing fluid retention—hence, the severe swelling—and putting undue stress on both me and our unborn child. The failure of my heart to adequately circulate blood could lead to devastating outcomes for both of us if not immediately addressed. By my side, Kenny held my hand, squeezing it tightly, as if he too needed an anchor in this turbulent sea of uncertainty.

Dr. Romano's professional composure was a softening note to the stark implications of my condition. Even as he said this, nurses attached me to machines that beeped and blinked, measuring my oxygen levels and the baby's heart rate. The medication to expedite our baby's lung development wasn't merely a precaution; it was vital. The supplemental oxygen wasn't just for my comfort; it was a necessity. It was all becoming too real.

When my parents entered the room, their eyes were filled with worry, underscoring that this was far from a typical night or a conventional Passover. The feast and prayers would have to wait. The swelling, the shortness of breath, the fatigue—all signs I had dismissed because my obstetrician had told me they were normal—had culminated in this precarious moment. My life and that of our unborn child hung in a delicate balance, cared for by medical professionals who were doing their best to tip the scales in our favor.

Despite Kenny's longing to stay, I insisted he go home and rest. We both knew he'd need his strength for whatever lay ahead. Our goodbye carried the weight of our unvoiced fears and hopes. Just as he exited, he crossed paths with Dr. Romano again. Tempted by the TV-drama atmosphere of it all, Kenny couldn't help but ask, "Is this going to be like an episode of *ER*?" Dr. Romano chuckled gently and assured Kenny that he didn't anticipate a made-for-television crisis. Little did we know our reality would be more gripping than any Emmy Award–winning scripted drama.

After a night of fragmented sleep, I awoke around 6:30 a.m., my mind whirring with anxiety and expectation. Limited to a quick trip to the bathroom, I returned to the confines of my hospital bed. And then it happened—a sudden gush of warm fluid flooded down my legs. Panic swallowed me whole, snuffing out any glimmer of rational thought. My fingers hammered the nurse call button. Frantically, I dialed Kenny on the bedside phone, my voice breaking as I sought his distant comfort.

The door swung open and nurses rushed into the room. Their faces were masks of professional calm, while my expression was one of abject terror. "You're in active labor," they told me, their words tinged with a hurried undertone. There was no time for pain relief; my body was accelerating faster than anyone had anticipated.

At thirty-two weeks pregnant, grappling with right congestive heart failure and enduring excruciating contractions, I was thrust into the unknown territory of labor. The timing was bitterly ironic; my prenatal classes were set to begin the next week, but I realized that no class could have truly equipped me for the raw and immediate reality I was facing. Fear gripped every fiber of my being and I felt utterly powerless. But deep down I knew I needed to focus on safeguarding the life growing within me. The well-being of the baby took precedence over my own. The intensity of the pain made it challenging to communicate coherently. Kenny's arrival was swift, defying all odds as he skillfully maneuvered through early morning city traffic to reach me in record time.

Surrounded by a flurry of doctors and nurses, my hospital room became a scene of immediacy. The ominous sound of "Code Blue" reverberated through the corridors, heightening the stakes. Amid whispered consultations and rapid-fire medical jargon, the option of transferring me to Toronto General Hospital surfaced—a place purportedly equipped to tackle my spiraling cardiac situation. The question "Who gets priority—the mother or the child?" sliced through the cacophony of beeping monitors and hurried footsteps. This was not an abstract ethical query; they were debating the course of my life and that of our unborn child. The air thickened, each word heavy with unbearable consequence.

Despite the pain coursing through my body, I clutched Kenny's shirt, mustering all my strength to assert my unwavering decision: "They are not to move me anywhere." I would deliver our baby at WCH, where its top-tier Neonatal Intensive Care Unit (NICU) could offer the best possible care. Kenny relayed my demand to the doctors, then assured me I would remain at WCH. In that moment, I felt disconnected from myself, observing the chaotic reality unfolding around me. The contractions surged relentlessly, rendering me speechless. The physical pain is a blur, but what remains vivid is that intuitive and profound conviction that, beneath the fear, *I would be okay*, just like when I was at Sick Kids for my leg surgery. I held on to the calm assurance that our baby and I would safely weather this tumultuous storm.

As I lay on the freezing table, the chill in the operating room clung to my skin like an unwanted guest. The pungent odor of disinfectant mingled with the slightly metallic aroma of blood, making the air taste clinical. Kenny, at my side, along with a nurse, grabbed my legs in an awkward embrace that served as makeshift stirrups. A moment of levity cut through the tension when the nurse playfully chided Kenny: "You're slacking! You need to keep her leg pulled back: it's your only job!" A ripple of laughter escaped my lips, a sensory break in an otherwise intense atmosphere, encouraging Kenny to up his game.

"Push!" The command hit like a crack of thunder, erasing all else. The world around me became a hazy blend of urgency and focus. I felt the gravitational pull of my entire being converge on this single moment. The baby was here—then carried out of my sight almost as quickly as they had arrived. My heart pounded in my ears, temporarily drowning out the chorus of medical chatter. I didn't even ask about the baby's sex; there was no room in my consciousness for that yet.

Seconds, which felt like an eternity, ticked by before the nurse declared, "It's a girl, and she's breathing on her own!" A flood of relief washed over me, so powerful that it tingled from the crown of my head to the tips of my toes. It was as if my entire body had exhaled. A salty tear slid past my lips; Kenny's face mirrored my own—elation and utter disbelief.

It was then that I sensed another presence: my mother. I hadn't been aware of her entering, but looking back, I'm convinced that I felt her strength enveloping me, another thread in this emotional web. On Friday, April 2, 1999, at 8:34 a.m., our daughter, Hannah Rubie, graced us with her presence, weighing a mere three pounds and seven ounces. From that moment, our lives were beautifully transformed.

Just when I thought the rollercoaster had come to a halt, my body convulsed in a surprising wave of contractions. My mind raced: *Could there be a second baby? A hidden twin?* The nurses quickly dispelled my confusion—or stupidity—educating me on the second act of childbirth: the placenta. Apparently, pushing out a human isn't enough; there's a freaking encore. The realization that I'd been so naive humbled me, even as I felt the pull of stitches mending an episiotomy[1] designed to spare my already strained heart.

Finally, the moment came. Tenderly, they placed Hannah in my arms—she was so delicate and petite. My senses were instantly filled with her: her warmth, the downy softness of her skin, and that indescribable scent that only newborns possess. It was love in its purest form—overwhelming, surreal, life-changing. It eclipsed every prior understanding I had of joy, engraving itself into the very core of my being. Kenny, at my side, joined me in this silent awe, our eyes brimming with emotion for the wonder we had just brought into the world.

After Hannah's birth, my heart began to stabilize. I was admitted to the ICU for close monitoring as doctors worked

---

[1] An episiotomy is a surgical incision made in the perineum, the area between the vagina and the anus, during childbirth to facilitate delivery and prevent tearing of the surrounding tissues. Source: Johns Hopkins Medicine, Health: Treatments, Tests and Therapies, "Episiotomy."

diligently to unravel the enigma of what had happened to me. All the while, I yearned to be with my daughter, who was two floors below me in the NICU. Nestled within an incubator that maintained her body temperature and mirrored the protection of a mother's womb, Hannah was secured to a feeding tube that provided her with the essential nutrients and hydration she wasn't yet able to ingest on her own. Kenny took a Polaroid picture of me, which he taped to her little isolette. Despite the difficult circumstances, I insisted that he dedicate most of his time to being with her, so she wouldn't feel alone or frightened. While I had complete trust in the exceptional care provided by the doctors and nurses in the neonatal unit, having Kenny by her side brought me an even greater sense of reassurance.

The ICU was a realm of chilling sterility and incessant beeping. I'll never forget that early morning when a nurse, in quiet defiance of protocol, wheeled Hannah, ensconced in her incubator, into my room. My fingers touched her tiny hand through the isolette's window, and the tears I couldn't contain came rushing down. This nurse understood that a mother needs her child and that their connection can be as healing as any medicine.

Once I was moved to the general cardiac floor, I was able to visit Hannah in the NICU—but I couldn't shake a lingering sense of guilt. I chastised myself for not heeding my body's earlier alerts, pondering if her premature birth could've been averted had I listened more closely. Desperate to make amends in some way, I ignored my own exhaustion and committed wholeheartedly to being there for her. I immersed myself in learning the intricacies of breastfeeding, became attuned to her subtle cues, and practiced skin-to-skin contact to offer her both warmth and emotional security. I believed this was my opportunity for redemption, a chance to regain some semblance of control in a situation that had been fraught with critical complexities.

A few days after the delivery, my acclaimed OB/GYN made her appearance. Referring to my early labor and her missing the birth, her first words to me, though in jest, were "What did you do to me?" Her humor did little to alleviate my anger, so intense that I struggled to even look at her. Despite holding myself accountable for dismissing my body's warning signs, I couldn't overlook the part she had played in neglecting those same signals. She hadn't truly listened to me as her patient, and her apparent lack of remorse was strikingly evident.

Eventually, once Hannah was safely home, I felt compelled to write to her. In my letter, I expressed my disappointment, not just seeking closure for myself but also hoping to impart a lesson from my experience that might encourage her to be more attentive to her current and future patients. Her reply was terse, a few lines absolving herself of any malpractice, coupled with well wishes. It was a succinct response, falling short of what I had anticipated, yet it allowed me to move forward and release my resentment.

After an exhausting month, which included ten days of my own hospitalization and a full month for Hannah in two different NICUs, we finally welcomed her home as she neared the five-pound milestone. This was an emotional amalgam: exuberance tinged with worry, jubilation shadowed by cautious optimism. The liberation we felt in leaving the hospital walls behind was coupled with the stark realization that we were now the sole guardians of this delicate new existence. Life doesn't request your permission to upend everything you thought you knew; it simply does, compelling you to adapt to your new normal. But it is in that very upheaval, in the process of unraveling and rebuilding, where transformation germinates. I emerged fortified: a mother imbued with a love both fierce and pure.

As Kenny and I established a rhythm with Hannah, our days and nights blended into a pattern of feeding, changing diapers, taking outdoor walks, and managing the countless other details of caring for a newborn. Kenny took on many of the early morning feedings, giving me precious time to rest. This shared responsibility laid new bricks in the ever-growing foundation of our family.

I found myself often hovering over her crib, watching her chest rise and fall, gently touching her delicate skin simply to feel her presence. Listening closely to her soft, contented murmurs and restless whimpers, I decoded the silent language of her needs. *Was she hungry? Was she wet?* Each check-in transformed into an intimate, wordless dialogue, a unique bond between mother and daughter.

Taking her for walks around the neighborhood was my parade of joy. Each step behind that carriage was a proclamation: "Look, world, this is Hannah—my greatest creation!" The rhythmic click-clack of stroller wheels against the pavement became a drumbeat, punctuating my newfound pride and purpose. Strangers would peer in to admire her, and with each smile or nod, I felt like I was collecting invisible badges of motherhood.

Even the sleepless nights—those soul-stretching marathons of constant feeding, changing, and comforting—included pockets of serenity. The moon would peek through the curtains as I rocked her, casting otherworldly patterns across her face. Her small hand would grasp my finger with surprising strength, and I'd feel a connection so primal and deep it was as though we were the only two spirits awake in a sleeping world. Despite the exhaustion that weighed on my eyelids and pulled at my bones, I savored those wee hours: a delicate weave of fatigue and elation, an array that chronicled our early evolution together.

You see, when you've stared down the abyss of almost losing the most precious part of you, every challenge becomes a gift. Each wail, each messy diaper, each bout of 3 a.m. colic is a reminder of what almost wasn't. It's as if facing my darkest fears had recalibrated my emotional compass, making me grateful for even the trials and tribulations of new motherhood. All of it—the ups and downs, the tears and the laughter—felt like hard-won grace. It was a poignant reminder of the extraordinary circumstances that made our ordinary moments nothing short of miraculous.

In both parenthood and running a marathon, I've learned to embrace the unpredictable twists and turns, to appreciate each high, and to glean wisdom from each low. So when I look back on these two defining experiences, I don't just see a birth and a race; I see a continuum of challenges and triumphs that have molded me into who I am today.

Dearest Reader: Have you ever found solace in the face of uncertainty? Where did this solace come from?

MILE 5

HHT

As I toed the starting line, the tension was palpable—I was a bundle of nerves. Among a sea of runners, I felt utterly alone with my thoughts. Months of grueling training had brought me here. Every bead of sweat, every strained muscle, every early morning wakeup was for this. Doubt washed over me. *Could I pull this off?* A soft but insistent voice from within replied, *I can do hard things.* Those words had already propelled me through miles of asphalt, each step a leap of faith, bringing me closer to a finish line that seemed both tantalizingly near and endlessly far away. Yet, the real depth of those words—*I can do hard things*—had a genesis far older, etched into my being more than two decades ago.

I vividly remember the day in May 1999 when I first met Dr. Marie Faughnan, a renowned respirologist who would become my guiding light through the complexities of my health. Referred from WCH, I was still contending with the unexplained right congestive heart failure that had cast a shadow over my pregnancy with Hannah.

I sat in her stuffy, cluttered office, the air thick with anxiety and expectation, as if it, too, was burdened by the weight of the news I was about to receive. Kenny was there, his hand a comforting pressure on my knee. Hannah lay peacefully in her bassinet car seat between us, blissfully unaware of how our lives were about to change. Dr. Faughnan, her own belly round with pregnancy, took her seat across from us. Her eyes met mine, locking into a gaze that felt like a bridge between two worlds. It was there, amid the unique juxtaposition of new life and looming diagnoses, that she confirmed what she had suspected: I had Hereditary Hemorrhagic Telangiectasia (HHT),[1] also known as Osler-Weber-Rendu Syndrome, a rare genetic disease wreaking havoc on my blood vessels.

She outlined the intricacy of my condition with an unsettling clarity. Venous malformations were lurking in my lungs and liver, like concealed landmines, setting the stage for my congestive heart failure. She pieced together the physiological puzzle that had baffled so many before her. My liver was essentially overworking my heart, sending torrents of blood through an organ not equipped for such a deluge. She revealed that even before I had become pregnant, my blood flow was akin to that of an expectant mother. The demands of pregnancy had then turned this issue into a critical problem, quadrupling my normal blood flow and stretching my heart's capabilities to its limits. This was the missing link, explaining the frightening swelling and breathlessness I had endured. The diagnosis hit me with a mix of relief and dread. Suddenly, the persistent nosebleeds that had been a recurring issue in my life—intensifying to the point of frighteningly uncomfortable emergency room visits during my pregnancy—gained a new, unsettling relevance.

---

[1] Hereditary Hemorrhagic Telangiectasia (HHT) is a rare genetic disorder affecting blood vessels. It leads to the formation of fragile, abnormal vessels that can bleed easily, manifesting as symptoms like nosebleeds and gastrointestinal bleeding. The condition can affect various organs, posing risks for more serious complications such as stroke. Sources: The National Institutes of Health and the Genetic and Rare Diseases Information Center.

As Dr. Faughnan informed us, I felt my world narrow, like the lens of a camera focusing on its subject. Her words carved out a chasm between my past and my future. I looked at my husband and daughter, the core of my newfound world, and my heart clenched with the thought: *Can I have more children?* When Dr. Faughnan's eyes met mine again, they seemed to hold the weight of my unspoken question. She mouthed a single, earth-shattering word: *No.*

The room blurred as I gazed at Hannah sleeping peacefully, unaware of the turmoil inside me. My heart felt heavy, like it was sinking into a pit I couldn't escape. Her existence, which should have been my greatest joy, now underscored an agonizing reality: she might be my only child. I was filled with love for her but ached knowing this might be the only time I'd experience this kind of love—would she be the only one whose first steps, first words, and first day of school I'd ever witness? That dream, that picture of a larger family, was suddenly gone, like a sandcastle swept away by a relentless tide.

In the claustrophobia of that moment, as the shadows of indecision and uncertainty stretched over me, my mind began to wander down different paths. *Adoption? It's a possibility, but who would guide us?* It felt like scaling a mountain. And then there was surrogacy. Deidre Hall, a name I'd only known from soap operas, suddenly flashed in my mind; she had chosen that path. I didn't know the ins and outs of surrogacy, but in that instant, I knew that my hope for a larger family wasn't entirely extinguished. The way forward might be clouded over, but my resolve to explore every avenue lit the road ahead.

A flood of questions churned inside me, each unanswered. *Whose life was this? Had I somehow brought this upon myself? Was there a lesson in all this?* At twenty-nine years old, with my life seemingly upended, all I could muster was a bewildered and heartbroken *Why me?*

Those subsequent months felt like an endless circuit within the confines of the hospital. Innumerable tests consumed my days, waiting in the bleak hallways of Wellesley Hospital and the recovery rooms that smelled of antiseptic and despair. HHT had turned my physiology into a chaotic landscape. I underwent angiographic pulmonary embolizations,[2] a term foreign to me until I experienced the procedure firsthand. Platinum coils were inserted into the damaged veins in my lungs to seal them off, which brought significant discomfort. Yet, the real agony set in during the recovery period, as the coiled veins—now deprived of blood—began to atrophy and scar. Coupled with the recent physical demands of motherhood, I felt as though I were wrestling with myself from the inside out. Through all this, Kenny stood beside me like a rock, even when I felt like a crumbling mess, riddled with guilt that I couldn't give him more children. A gnawing emptiness persisted.

With family and friends, we were an open book about my HHT diagnosis—but the inability to have more children? That was a secret chapter we weren't ready to publish. The emotional gravity of it was just too heavy to be laid bare.

---

[2] Angiographic pulmonary embolization is a procedure used to treat abnormal blood vessels in the lungs by blocking them off. A catheter is guided through the blood vessels to the site of the abnormality, and embolic agents are released to obstruct the blood flow, effectively eliminating the problematic area. Source: The Cleveland Clinic's Health Library, Treatments & Procedures, "Embolization."

HHT isn't in the past; it's an ever-present undertow in the sea of my life. Dr. Faughnan, now at St. Michael's Hospital, remains my compass. Every six months, I step into the familiar halls of St. Mike's for a series of tests on my heart, lungs, and liver. It's a routine that harbors both reassurance and a flicker of foreboding. I've grown acutely aware that any of these visits could bring a shift, a deviation from the normalcy I've come to know. I welcome the moments I can step out of that hospital with a semi-annual respite ahead of me. Dr. Faughnan has been by my side for a quarter of a century. I trust her implicitly, so before I even thought about tackling something as strenuous as a marathon, her opinion, along with my cardiologist's, was a prerequisite. They both gave me a cautious green light, fully aware of the monumental challenge ahead. That then set off nine months of hard training, a period of pushing my body's boundaries while always mindful of its limitations. As with everything else in my life, it was a delicate balancing act.

Life has its marathons and its "diagnosis" rooms, its starting lines and its dead ends. But in these diverging paths, I've found an unwavering constant: *I can do hard things.* And, dearest reader, as you walk with me through the pages of my life, know that you are never alone in your journey. We can do hard things. And often, it's those very things that reveal who we truly are.

Dearest Reader: How has resilience and the belief in your own strength guided you through the complexities of life's unexpected challenges?

MILE 6

TRAINING AND TRAILS

For me, running is not merely a sequence of rhythmic footfalls; it's a transcendent gateway for the soul. The communion of my feet with the earth below me, as if part of an unspoken covenant, fills me with joy. Yet, running is not without its trials. The moments when quitting seems most tempting are precisely those that force me to summon my inner grit. It's a nudge to respect both the mind and body.

My love affair with running has spanned well over two decades, but the fall of 1998, when I was twenty-seven, stands out as a seminal point. Participating in a charity 6.2-mile (10 km) event in Toronto marked a notable shift. The rhythm of running wasn't foreign to me, but the intimidating distance was uncharted territory. As I began training, my body often rebelled, questioning this newfound ambition. *Who genuinely enjoys this madness?* Yet, as the weeks progressed, the post-run euphoria became more pronounced. The surge of endorphins became something I eagerly anticipated. My legs, though tired, resonated with a sense of accomplishment. And beneath that weariness, I held on to a quiet pride, knowing I had pushed myself just a little further, one step at a time.

As my forty-ninth birthday neared, I began toying with the notion of a momentous challenge. The concept of running a major marathon crystallized in my mind—a symbol of personal power and an affirmation of what one can achieve. It felt like the ideal celebration, a testament to endurance and spirit, to usher in the milestone of half a century. However, the outbreak of COVID-19 disrupted those plans, spreading uncertainty worldwide. By February 2022, as society emerged from the pandemic, the dream of running the marathon rekindled. That's when I decided to register for the NYC Marathon scheduled for November 2022. Shifting from a manageable 6.2 miles (10 km) to an intimidating 26.2 miles (42.2 km) necessitated a different approach. With the ever-present limitations of HHT lurking in the shadows, every step had to be measured. After extensive research, I crafted a training regimen. Kenny became my reliable ally, not only helping map out my trails but also pedaling beside me on his bike during my more demanding runs—ostensibly for companionship but truly to ensure I wasn't jeopardizing my health by overexerting myself. His constant presence made each mile more bearable and every challenge less intimidating, reinforcing the belief that we were, indeed, better together.

Running, at times, is a paradox of emotions—a love/hate relationship that intertwines reluctance and satisfaction. Some mornings, my shoes assume the heft of anchors, and the prospect of another run feels daunting. Yet, it's during these moments of doubt that the spirit of training truly unveils itself. It's not just about physical endurance but also about conquering the mind's trepidation.

The essence of a marathon isn't captured solely on the day of the race. It's in the relentless hours of training, the diverse routes explored, and the varying terrains braved. My own odyssey ushered me through the lush greenery of Toronto's parks and the rugged trails of Northern Ontario. These solo runs transformed into moving meditations. Podcasts guided my initial pace, but eventually the driving rhythms of my curated playlists took over, propelling me forward. Impactful as those solitary runs were, nothing could truly simulate or prepare me for the electrifying atmosphere that awaited me in the urban landscape of New York City.

    Navigating Brooklyn's lively streets, I drew energy from the enthusiastic crowd. Their cheers seemed to elevate me, each step lighter than the last. Each borough offered its unique brand of local enthusiasm, surpassing anything I'd envisioned. But as I neared the Queensboro Bridge entrance, the atmosphere shifted dramatically. Just beyond the 15-mile (24.1 km) mark, the exhilaration of Queens yielded to the silent expanse of the bridge. With each step I took, the clamor of the spectators faded, replaced by the rhythmic cadence of my own shoes on the bridge's surface. This almost mile-long stretch offered a precious gift: solitude. It was a moment to reconnect with myself, welcome self-reflection, and tap into that well of inner strength.

    As I descended from the bridge, the cheers that awaited me on Manhattan's First Avenue sent vibrations through my soul, evoking the thrill of a home run in Yankee Stadium. In that mass of spectators, their faces filling the sides of the road, I sought out my supporting family, my intuition guiding my gaze. Just at the edge of my vision, I saw them. Veering quickly, I shared a fleeting moment, assuring them of my well-being. Their mere presence was uplifting, reminding me I wasn't on this journey alone. Galvanized by their confidence, I surged ahead with renewed vigor, the finish line drawing nearer with every step, now just 10 miles (16 km) away.

Dearest Reader: When have you paused to truly immerse yourself in the now, letting the moment engulf you? What did it reveal?

MILE 7

THE ROAD TO SURROGACY

When I contemplate the beginning of our surrogacy journey, the poignant words of Robert Frost come to mind: "Two roads diverged in a wood, and I—I took the one less traveled by, and that has made all the difference."[1]

During Hannah's first year, not every day was fairy-tale perfect, but many moments shimmered with a certain magic. Her petite frame housed a wellspring of remarkable strength that revitalized my spirit amid inner turmoil. The gut-wrenching reality of not being able to bear more children weighed on me, yet my daughter's presence acted as a counterbalance, infusing lightness into my days. From weekly music gatherings with other new mothers to our animated Gymboree classes, we were an inseparable pair.

As for my health, it was average at best. I continued to undergo numerous procedures to mitigate the adverse effects of HHT. Medical interventions became necessary routine pitstops.

A year into our new rhythm, news of second pregnancies among friends and acquaintances started reaching my ears. It was a bittersweet pill to swallow. I had already started to research the labyrinthine world of surrogacy and was coming

---

[1] These lines of poetry are from "The Road Not Taken" by Robert Frost, published in his collection *Mountain Interval*, 1916.

to grips with its complexity and demands. It felt akin to the first day of training for a marathon, feeling overwhelmed and unsure. *Where should I begin? What knowledge am I lacking? Where can I find the information I need?*

The well-meaning comments from family members often carried a lingering bite, their intended comfort sometimes feeling like subtle jabs: "Isn't one healthy baby enough?" or "Many are content with just one." Yet every reminder to "count my blessings" only deepened the ache and amplified the whispering voice within that I wasn't whole yet.

As I embarked on this road with limited knowledge, I grasped the fundamental idea: surrogacy involves one woman carrying a baby for another. While today, surrogacy has gained recognition through celebrity stories and advancements in fertility technology, when we began twenty-five years ago, it was shrouded in silence.

There are two main types of surrogacy: traditional and gestational. In traditional surrogacy, the surrogate mother is also the biological mother of the child. She becomes pregnant through insemination with sperm from the intended father or a donor. In gestational surrogacy, the situation is different: the surrogate mother carries a baby that has no genetic connection to her. The child is conceived through in vitro fertilization (IVF),[2] where eggs from the intended mother or a donor are fertilized by sperm from the intended father or a donor. The resulting embryo is then transferred to the surrogate's uterus.

---

[2] In vitro fertilization (IVF) is a procedure in which eggs are collected and fertilized by sperm outside the body in a laboratory. The resulting embryo is transferred into the uterus to establish a pregnancy. IVF is one of the most well-known assisted reproductive technologies used to overcome infertility. Source: The Mayo Clinic's Health Library, Tests & Procedures, "In vitro fertilization (IVF)."

In our case, we opted for gestational surrogacy, using my eggs and Kenny's sperm.

I was disheartened to discover that information on surrogacy in Canada was scant until I stumbled upon an agency in Southern Ontario led by Mary, a woman who had herself walked this path as a surrogate. Our conversations were raw and honest, shedding light on the true costs, legal maze, and myriad of emotions—both challenging and rewarding—that came with surrogacy. Mary's immense empathy filled me with renewed confidence. I remember asking her, my voice shaky, if we'd ever have another baby. She looked at me with eyes that seemed to have seen countless stories like mine and whispered, "It's not about *if*, but *when*." In that moment, a fire of determination was kindled within me—one I hadn't felt in ages.

Kenny and I often lost ourselves in thoughtful conversations about our path forward. There wasn't any tension or dissent about the expenses or its impact on our financial horizon. Reflecting on those days, a warm gratitude washes over me. I had an equal partner who, without hesitation, handed me the reins to our shared quest for a larger family.

We decided to engage Mary's services and sought her assistance in finding a gestational surrogate in Ontario. It's crucial to note that laws and regulations surrounding surrogacy vary significantly by country. Legal complexities can arise concerning the status of the surrogate mother, the rights and responsibilities of the intended parents, and the child's rights. Surrogacy is legal in Canada but subject to specific regulations. The Assisted Human Reproduction Act (AHRA) and its corresponding regulations govern surrogacy in Canada. According to the AHRA, commercial surrogacy—where money exchanges hands beyond reimbursement for the surrogate's reasonable expenses—is prohibited. However, it's important to note that "reasonable expenses" can be a gray area, and many intended parents find ways to adequately compensate their surrogates within the bounds of the law.

Traversing the multifaceted world of fertility in Toronto was overwhelming, and we consulted numerous experts to find the best chance for success. As we committed to this path, we also partnered with a surrogacy attorney, solidifying our resolve. Not all doctors in the city were open to working with gestational surrogates, with legal nuances clouding the practice. Then we met Dr. Lee Crosse. His office, a testament to his many successes, was lined with baby photos and heartfelt thank-you notes. Despite these cheery visuals, the space itself lacked a certain warmth, feeling more like a clinical showcase than a welcoming doctor's office. However, beyond the aesthetics, it was his conveyance of genuine hope that truly drew us in. Dr. Crosse, often with elusive eyes, presented a demeanor that, in any other situation, might have prompted greater scrutiny. But my sense of desperation was dulled by the confidence he exuded, steering me to lean on his judgment rather than question it.

At the beginning, we often heard the brighter side: stories of triumph, advanced technology, and the allure of guaranteed success. Dr. Crosse made us feel that our path would be smooth, and given that our challenges weren't rooted in fertility, achievement seemed almost inevitable. But as with any journey, there were layers, subtleties, and truths that perhaps in our eagerness we overlooked. At the time, I didn't hear about the disparities between reproductive technologies in the United States and Canada. I didn't know that birth statistics don't always reflect live birth rates. I didn't realize that there is no unified governing body in Canada to ensure fertility clinics provide accurate accounts of their actual live birth rates.

Confronting the world of fertility is more than just medical protocols and hopeful stories; it's a test of spirit and resilience. Nobody prepares you for the sharp, intimate sting of needles as they puncture your skin daily, sometimes multiple times. These injections aren't just a physical ordeal; they're laden with hormones meant to boost your egg development, altering not just your body but also your emotional state. They transform your biology. The egg retrieval is clinical, brutally so, and the ache is raw and utterly unyielding. Every suction, every wrench at your ovaries—you don't just feel it; you grit your teeth and bear it. After all the invasive interventions and the seemingly endless wait, when you're holding on to every fragment of hope, a negative pregnancy test isn't just disappointing—it's a visceral punch. It's a profound heartbreak that often remains unspoken.

When desperation takes hold, questions tend to fade away, and you simply accept what the doctor tells you, driven by the palpable anguish and the unwavering desire to succeed. Much like my pregnancy with Hannah, I once again placed my trust in another's expertise, naively accepting every word as gospel. *How many times must one repeat a lesson before it truly takes hold?* Reflecting on this brings a rueful smile to my face. Without the whirlwind of challenges, heartaches, and hurdles, I wouldn't be where I am now. Our surrogacy journey, turbulent as it was, feels in hindsight like it was our destined route. And that deep-seated belief endowed it with an immutable sense of fate.

Throughout it all, I maintained a straightforward, unembellished journal. This was an unvarnished, real-time chronicle of our tribulations and aspirations, a document I wanted our children to read one day. It would help them understand the unfiltered love that we have for them, even before their conception. In it, I didn't hold back—I spilled every frustration, setback, and heartbreak but also the bursts of hope, tenacity, and hard-won victories.

The following italicized excerpts reproduced here have been lightly edited, although the authentic tone stands.

May 30, 2000

If you're reading this, it means our dream has come true: we've succeeded in bringing you into this world. These pages won't just record events; they'll capture the optimism, challenges, and undeniable love that have been part of your story from the very start. This is where it begins.

Dearest Reader: What raw, unfiltered narratives are you writing in your own life's journey?

MILE 8

TOO GOOD TO BE TRUE

With the help of Mary's expertise, we were matched with Amy, a dental hygienist living just outside of Toronto who had a teenage son. This was particularly reassuring, as reputable surrogacy agencies in the U.S. and Canada stipulate that surrogates must have previously given birth. This policy has a dual purpose: it aids in managing potential emotional connections more effectively and ensures that the surrogate comprehends the full spectrum of the physical and psychological demands involved in maintaining a healthy pregnancy. Knowing that Amy had met this essential criterion provided us with a sense of initial comfort as we embarked on this multifarious process.

Experiencing surrogacy firsthand unveiled a great insight: it's not just about the science of conception, but the intricate dance of human connection. Placing trust in someone you've only recently met to nurture and carry a life for nine months is a tremendous leap of faith. In my initial conversation with Amy, the topics were far from casual. We navigated sensitive and emotional terrain as we discussed not just the logistics of ultrasounds and vaginal births but also touched on the delicate issue of abortion. We were, in effect, entrusting each other with deeply personal revelations and sharing vulnerabilities, all in the hope of forming a partnership that would eventually result in a new life.

When the day arrived for us to meet face to face, the atmosphere of the downtown Toronto coffee shop was heavy with unspoken questions. Kenny, Mary, and I looked up in anticipation as the bell above the door chimed and Amy walked in. She was taller than I'd imagined, her casual jeans and graphic tee broadcasting a laidback confidence. The moment she sat down, all the weight lifted. Laughter filled the gaps between our nervous sips of coffee. In the way our eyes met and lingered was the shared realization that we were all thinking about the same binding commitment. By the time we parted, the sense of optimism building throughout our meeting had solidified into a mutual understanding: we were ready to begin this remarkable undertaking together.

With Mary's help, the tangled web of medical and legal requirements became more clear. She led us through each step meticulously, from mapping out the necessary health screenings to guiding Amy toward seeking specialized legal counsel for surrogates.

Next, we found ourselves at Dr. Crosse's clinic, fortified with information and each other's support.

For our initial foray into in vitro fertilization, we chose a more natural course—I would abstain from fertility medications. The health risks associated with taking fertility meds because of my HHT were something I needed to consider. The strategy unfolded, starting with an egg retrieval procedure.[1] In this delicate process, Dr. Crosse used a specialized needle, guided by ultrasound imaging, to carefully extract an egg from one of my ovaries. Although I experienced some discomfort, the anticipation of the potential outcome rendered the experience manageable. Following the retrieval, the next phase took place within the confines of a laboratory. There, my egg was combined with Kenny's sperm to create an embryo. The final, critical step involved the precise implantation of this embryo into Amy's uterus. For this, a catheter—a slender, flexible instrument—was used, its placement also directed by ultrasound to ensure optimal positioning.

Kenny's part in this intricate medical protocol? A racy magazine, a sterilized cup, and *boom*—in less than three minutes, he's done! The miracles of modern fertility science never ceased to amaze.

June 15, 2000

> *When I heard Amy's voice through the phone, the air in the room seemed to vibrate. "Are you sitting down?" she cautioned, a little thrill in her tone. "You're having another baby!" At that instant, my heart pounded against my ribcage, a tsunami of exhilaration and disbelief. Was I in a state of shock or euphoria? It was impossible to tell.*
>
> *I had to share the news immediately. As I dialed Kenny's number, my fingers trembled. "You might want to sit down,"*

---

[1] Egg retrieval, part of the IVF process, involves using a needle guided by ultrasound to collect eggs from the ovaries for fertilization in a lab. Source: The Mayo Clinic's Health Library, Tests & Procedures, "Egg-retrieval technique."

I echoed Amy's words, sensing his attention snap into focus. "We're going to have another baby, we're pregnant!" There was a pause on the other end—a vacuum where time seemed to freeze—before his voice returned, reflecting my own sense of awe.

As the news settled in, my mind fast-forwarded to early March 2001. It felt almost dreamlike to think that we'd be welcoming a new life into our family, elevating Hannah to the role of a big sister. Astonishingly, we'd defied the odds, conceiving on our first attempt without the aid of fertility medications.

<u>June 23, 2000</u>

Things are progressing well, and containing our joy is becoming a delightful challenge. The thrill was electric when we broke the news to our families; jubilation filled the air.

Amy and I communicate almost every other day. With five weeks since the embryo transfer, the anticipation for the first ultrasound at 6.5 weeks is mounting. Amy's consistently rising Human Chorionic Gonadotropin (hCG)[2] levels, as confirmed by her latest blood tests, only heighten our hopeful outlook.

Though there's a part of me that wishes circumstances allowed me to carry this child, knowing Amy is giving herself the best

---

[2] Human Chorionic Gonadotropin (hCG), a hormone produced during pregnancy, is detected through a blood test around eleven days after conception and continues to rise, usually peaking around eight to eleven weeks into the pregnancy. Source: The Cleveland Clinic's Health Library, Articles, "<u>Human Chorionic Gonadotropin</u>."

possible care offers a deep sense of reassurance. Daily, my thoughts drift toward our unborn child and the day we can welcome them into our arms.

July 4, 2000

Today felt surreal, a mix of nerves and hope as we sat in the ultrasound room. The cold gel was smoothed over Amy's belly, a prelude to what would be a morning we'd never forget. She lay on the table, a small smile crossing her lips as the doctor began the scan.

The room seemed to hold its breath, with only the soft whir of the ultrasound machine and the muffled thump-thump heartbeat from the monitor to be heard. And then it happened: not one but two distinct heartbeats filled the room, as if announcing, "We're here, and we're real." Identical twins. The odds felt almost astronomical—a single fertilized egg, now two miraculous lives.

We're only 6.5 weeks into this pregnancy, and we're aware that anything can happen. Yet, hearing those two heartbeats felt monumental: a blend of awe and humble vulnerability. A storm of emotions washed over us—elation, anxiety, and an indescribable sense of being intricately connected to something far greater than ourselves. Now more than ever we rely on Amy to create the caring atmosphere essential for the growth of our babies.

July 9, 2000

As I sit in the quietude of my family's cottage in Northern Ontario, surrounded by the vast lake and the untouched wilderness, nature's stillness envelops me. Here, where the air is pure and time seems to slow, the only sounds are the gentle lapping of water against the dock and the distant calls of wildlife. In this peaceful haven, my thoughts, paradoxically, are far from calm.

Thursday is approaching, and with it comes our second ultrasound. The mere thought of seeing those two tiny forms on the screen sends jolts of excitement through me. This is becoming less of an abstract idea and more of a touchable reality. Can you believe it? Soon, I'll be wrangling three kids under the age of two.

At night, just before sleep claims me, and in the morning, when the world is starting to wake up, my thoughts circle back to those babies. They're seven weeks and a day in the making, and yet they're already so real in my heart. Of course, I keep my feet on the ground; it's still early days. But it's hard not to drift into daydreams—imagining first steps, first words, the chaotic and beautiful life that awaits us. They fill my thoughts, stir my emotions, and fan the flames of hope and wonder. And for now, that's more than enough.

Thursday, July 13, 2000

We miscarried, and the pain is indescribable.

Dearest Reader: What event in your life made you confront the fragility of hope and the harsh reality of despair?

PART II

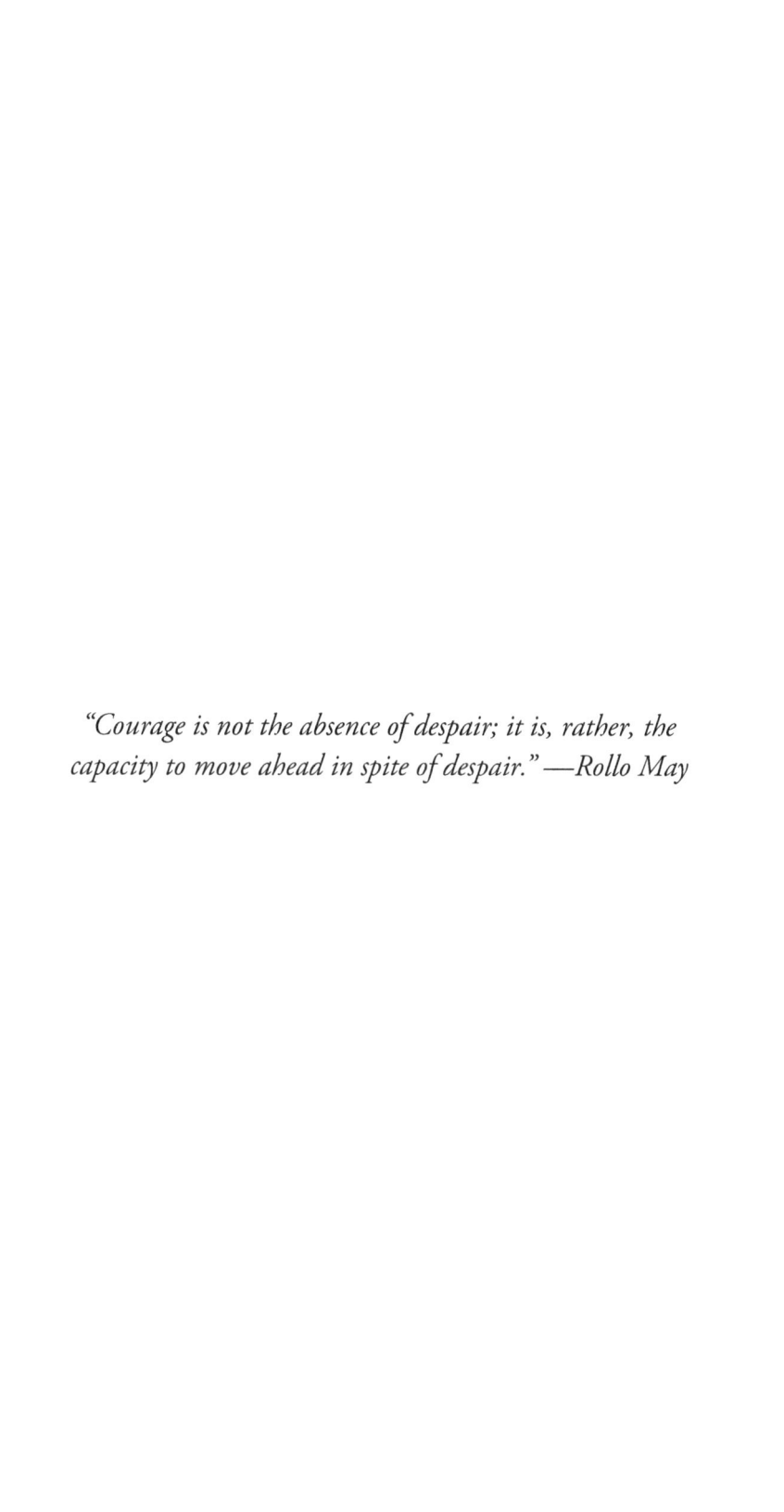

"Courage is not the absence of despair; it is, rather, the capacity to move ahead in spite of despair." —Rollo May

MILE 9

DISILLUSION AND DISAPPOINTMENT

In life, we advance through a series of invisible mile markers—moments that, in retrospect, help define our journey, such as graduations and career moves, getting married and becoming parents. Significant events like these often gain their full meaning only when we have the distance of time and experience to look back and understand how they shaped us.

In the world of long-distance running, mile markers are physical objects strategically placed along the route as signs of both how far you've come and how much farther you have to go. Every marker is a checkpoint that poses a silent looming question: *Do you have the stamina to keep going or do you need to stop and reassess?* Each one can be a moment of triumph, a rush of adrenaline fueling you forward, or a wall that you hit, forcing you to dig deep into reserves you didn't know you had.

This idea of mile markers can be remarkably apt when thinking about surrogacy—a complex process full of hope and dread, expectation and disappointment. Each phase in my and Kenny's experience served as its own concrete milestone in our quest toward having another baby: the hormone-altering fertility medications, the tense waits in the doctors' offices, the hopeful expectations before getting a pregnancy test result. And much like a marathoner gauging energy reserves, each step in the fertility journey prompts a poignant decision: *Do we push forward or take a breather? Do we dare to aspire or should we brace for impact?* Some of these mile markers have brought us closer to our dreams, infusing us with renewed purpose and determination. Others have been punishing, leaving us to question the viability of our hopes. Yet, at each point, we've had to make a choice: stop, go, pause, leap. Each choice, in turn, defining the contours of our story.

Following our miscarriage, Amy underwent a dilation and curettage (D&C)[1] procedure. While I didn't harbor resentment or blame toward her for the loss, I sometimes wondered if she had done everything possible to maintain her well-being, sidestepping strenuous activities and prolonged standing. The feeling of helplessness over something so personal was overwhelming. We never really discussed it, preferring instead to redirect our focus forward, steering our expectations and energies toward the forthcoming attempt.

I underwent another round of natural egg extraction, but the embryo proved to be nonviable for transfer. As October arrived, it was time to shift gears, and with unwavering resolve, I prepared myself for the fertility protocol. The daily regimen

---

[1] Dilation and curettage (D&C) is a procedure in which the cervix is dilated and the lining of the uterus is scraped to remove tissue. Source: The American College of Obstetricians and Gynecologists, "Dilation and Curettage (D&C)."

of Lupron[2] injections for three solid weeks (a necessary grind to control my estrogen levels), alongside the daily Puregon[3] shots to stimulate the growth of my eggs, was nothing short of brutal. Dr. Crosse noted the encouraging development of my follicles, a silver lining in the taxing process. The swelling of my ovaries was impossible to ignore. It was as if I was carrying heavy orbs deep within, their presence marked by a constant, throbbing ache. Each movement, subtle or pronounced, echoed their existence, a testament to the profound changes my body was undergoing. (At least this time the swelling was internal, a contrast to the udder-like expansion of my labia during my pregnancy with Hannah.)

Gatorade, which helped balance my electrolytes, was a must-have component of my fertility treatments. It counteracted some side effects of the cocktail of medications and injections flooding my system, in particular the risk of ovarian hyperstimulation,[4] a condition where the ovaries can swell and leak fluid. As I trained for the marathon,

---

[2] Lupron is a medication commonly used to regulate hormones in conditions ranging from prostate cancer to endometriosis and is frequently employed in fertility treatments to control ovarian stimulation. It reduces the production of certain hormones, such as estrogen and testosterone. Source: Drugs.com, "Lupron Depot."

[3] Puregon (also known as follitropin beta) is a medication often used in fertility treatments to stimulate the development of ovarian follicles in women and to increase sperm production in men. It is a synthetic form of the naturally occurring follicle-stimulating hormone (FSH). Source: Drugs.com, "Puregon."

[4] Ovarian Hyperstimulation Syndrome (OHSS) is a rare but potential side effect of fertility treatments, particularly those involving hormone injections to stimulate egg production. It can cause symptoms such as abdominal swelling, pain, nausea, and, in severe cases, more serious health issues. Source: The Cleveland Clinic's Health Library, Diseases & Conditions, "Ovarian Hyperstimulation Syndrome (OHSS)."

that same Gatorade took on a different role. Although it was now fueling my muscles and hydrating my body for a physical challenge, each sip was an immediate recollection of my past fertility struggles. Even after all those years, the flavor instantly transported me back to that emotional, nerve-racking time. It was a powerful reminder that the challenges of the past are always a part of us, even as we keep racing forward.

The egg retrieval felt like an assault. Lying on that unforgiving steel table, anxiety coursed through me, matching the chill of the metal. My legs hoisted in stirrups left me feeling bare and exposed. The Ativan they gave me took the edge off, but hardly. There was no anesthesiologist to offer further relief, and Dr. Crosse's efforts to numb my cervix seemed only superficial; every suction, every extraction from my ovaries reverberated sharply within me. Out of the eighteen eggs harvested, ten were successfully fertilized. Dr. Crosse suggested we transfer three embryos to boost our chances. We were wrestling with how much risk to take. The possibility of selective reduction (also known as fetal reduction),[5] a procedure contemplated when multiple embryos develop to a level that might endanger the pregnancy or the health of the gestational carrier, weighed heavily on our minds. We grappled with the profound ethical and emotional implications involved. Yet, Dr. Crosse, ever the clinician,

---

[5] Selective reduction or fetal reduction is a procedure used in fertility treatments to decrease the number of fetuses in a multiple pregnancy, improving the chances of a successful, healthy pregnancy and birth. It's often considered in cases of high-order multiple pregnancies (triplets or more) to reduce the risk of pregnancy complications. Source: inviTRA, "Multifetal pregnancy reduction – the how and why of the procedure."

was steadfast in his belief that increasing the number of transferred embryos was our best shot.

Three embryos were transferred to Amy's uterus, while the seven others were cryopreserved[6] (frozen) at the clinic for future use. The decision wasn't easy, but the doctor's reassurances echoed in our ears: if circumstances demanded, one embryo could be reduced without jeopardizing the others.

Amy took a home pregnancy test before her scheduled blood work for Sunday, October 22, and the result was negative. With each passing hour, my heart grew heavier at the looming possibility that the outcome might not change.

My primary worry was about how many embryos to transfer, blindsided by the notion that three healthy ones might not guarantee a pregnancy. The fear of triplets felt like a distant, misplaced concern now. The universe's unexpected turn stung acutely. Many nights tears would soak my pillow, and I sent fervent prayers skyward, yearning for a different result. Every setback felt like an immense void, magnifying the emotional, physical, and financial toll this journey demanded.

Upon hearing the news that there was no pregnancy, my mind swirled with disbelief. *How had three robust embryos, set in a healthy environment, not thrived?* The disappointment was heavy.

Before we could embark on another attempt, we were drawn into a waiting game. Amy's cycle was the starting point, and the next transfer was scheduled for about ten to twelve days later, pushing us into November. During this

---

[6] Embryo cryopreservation is a common practice in IVF treatments. Embryos that are not used in the initial IVF cycle can be frozen and stored for future use. Source: Wikipedia, "Embryo cryopreservation."

time, Kenny and I found ourselves striking a delicate balance. We communicated openly and regularly, discussing what steps we could take to improve the chances of a successful transfer. Life continued in its usual flow—Kenny dove into his work and I spent my days with Hannah—yet, beneath the surface of these familiar scenes, there was a distinct sense of dual existence. While our daily routine continued with its comforting cadence and small joys, we also lived in a state of watchful anticipation, the upcoming start of Amy's cycle casting a quiet, pervasive sense of expectancy over everything.

I was only beginning to grasp the sheer complexity and the number of obstacles this journey would present. Surrendering was not an option.

Dr. Crosse couldn't pinpoint the exact reason our IVF had failed. Instead, he encouraged us to look forward, reminding us of the seven embryos we still had in reserve, with plans to transfer another three into Amy. Despite this reassurance, a small seed of contingency began to sprout in my mind. I was contemplating the feasibility of consulting with clinics in the U.S., where success rates were reportedly higher, albeit paired with a heftier financial commitment.

Amy had voiced that if this attempt didn't take, she wished to grant her body a well-deserved break, hoping to resume anew in January. The gravity of the entire situation and its ever-extending timeline was becoming a substantial burden on my shoulders. During a routine checkup, my family doctor saw my struggle and proposed I seek therapy. While Kenny remained my pillar of support, he was my only confidant through these turbulent emotions. The idea of hearing from an impartial voice to affirm that I wasn't losing myself in the chaos seemed like a necessary step.

Amid everything, a fellow mom from Hannah's music class called to let me know she was pregnant with her second child. The physical distance a phone call afforded was a blessing, as it felt like a swift, jarring blow, leaving me breathless. Watching someone else's life progress in the very direction you long for is a difficult reality to accept. In moments such as this, it felt as though I was trapped in a persistent cycle, spinning endlessly, craving for my own narrative of fulfillment.

Engaging in therapy was thoroughly beneficial for me. Regina, though petite in stature, exuded a commanding presence. Her office was a kaleidoscope of colors, an inviting mix of organized clutter. Books were littered around, and the ambiance brought a grin to my face. Through her large window, a serene-looking garden was visible.

With every session, I felt I was unburdening a part of my soul. It was there that I faced the raw, wrenching grief of acknowledging that I would never bear another child. Regina listened, her eyes echoing back my pain, validating every tear and tremor of my voice. She made me understand that grieving the loss of a dream was just as real as mourning a tangible loss.

Time and again, well-intentioned family members would point out the blessings I already possessed, insinuating that it should quell my desire for another child. Yet, what my heart truly craved was empathy from those around me. Not to overshadow the blessings I was already thankful for, but to see the deep-seated pain I carried and to grant me the space to mourn.

As I left Regina's office after our sessions, the weight seemed a bit lighter. The path ahead might hold its share of thorns, but I walked on, fortified with a renewed faith, a resilient belief that our family's story was still unfolding, with chapters of joy awaiting us.

November 12, 2000

I feel a surge of hope at the core of my being. There's something distinct about this transfer; it resonates differently. Yesterday's procedure was seamless. It met with the doctor's genuine satisfaction as the three embryos thawed and divided with promise. Our surrogate is also in an ideal state, well-rested and with no imminent return to work.

In hushed contemplation, I envision two embryos finding their place, and in those moments, I channel every ounce of strength and hope toward them. A firmly seated conviction stirs within me that this time, it will happen. Our enduring dreams stand at the cusp of becoming real.

November 22, 2000

Every evening, Kenny and I sit on our bedroom floor. We light a single candle, its glow barely enough to illuminate our faces but sufficient to cast away the darkness. There's a charge in the air—the kind that lingers around things that matter deeply. We join hands, our fingers interlocking as if trying to meld our very hopes together. It's in this moment that we silently acknowledge the weight of our shared wish: that Amy is pregnant. She's cautiously optimistic that she's pregnant, and we can't help but mirror her sentiment. And each night, as we unclasp our hands and extinguish the candle, the darkness feels a little less daunting, replaced by a growing light of possibility.

<u>November 24, 2000</u>

The pregnancy test came back negative. I remind myself to "believe."

Dearest Reader: Have you ever wrestled with the balance between acknowledging blessings and allowing yourself to grieve for unfulfilled dreams?

MILE 10

CHASING MIRACLES

It seemed that each day another person in my circle was sharing their pregnancy news. I knew I had to stop measuring my journey against theirs. Kenny and I consulted an infertility specialist, who enlightened us about the distinctions between Canadian fertility practices and some of the top-tier clinics in the United States. Interestingly, she had overcome her own challenges with fertility, eventually conceiving twin boys with the assistance of a clinic in Denver, Colorado. While her perspective might have been slightly biased toward U.S. clinics, my own investigations began to underline why they were held in such high regard. The live birth rates at the Denver clinic were notably higher than the ones at the clinic we were working with. Yes, the costs were steeper, but we wanted to optimize our chance for success.

Over the past two decades, the regulatory landscape and measures for transparency within the fertility clinic industry in Canada and the United States have evolved, while also maintaining foundational structures. In the early 2000s, regulations were present but lacked the uniformity and comprehensiveness observed today.

In Canada, the governance of fertility clinics has traditionally been managed by individual provinces, leading to diverse regulatory frameworks across the nation. This has resulted in varying standards and practices from one region to another. Despite changes aimed at improving transparency and standardizing operations, provincial responsibility continues to guide the functioning of Canadian fertility clinics, preserving the regional discrepancies in regulation.

Similarly, in the United States, the regulatory landscape has traditionally been characterized by state-specific rules, resulting in varied standards and requirements for fertility clinics. While there have been shifts toward greater transparency and uniformity, state-specific regulations remain central, continuing to produce a diverse set of guidelines across the country.

Amid these evolving regulatory frameworks, organizations such as the Canadian Fertility and Andrology Society (CFAS) and the U.S.'s Society for Assisted Reproductive Technology (SART) have played pivotal roles. Both organizations have been instrumental in collecting and publishing data on clinic success rates, contributing to increased transparency and informing patient decisions. These efforts by CFAS and SART represent considerable strides toward standardizing practices and enhancing patient knowledge, even as the overarching regulatory structures remain anchored in regional governance.

The interaction between evolving standards and enduring regional oversight highlights the dynamic nature of fertility clinic regulation in both Canada and the U.S., underscoring ongoing efforts to balance localized control with the push for broader standardization and transparency in the fertility industry.

Our next appointment with Dr. Crosse was meant to be a simple checkpoint. But with the revelations about the Denver clinic fresh in our minds, Kenny and I saw this as the perfect opportunity to discuss a potential shift.

Walking into his consultation room, a discernible tension hung in the air. When we broached the Denver topic, he reacted unexpectedly: surprised with a touch of hurt. "Why Denver?" Dr. Crosse asked, a note of disbelief in his voice.

Determined, I presented our findings, emphasizing the impressive live birth rates and accolades of the Denver clinic. But as I continued, his discomfort became unmistakable. He ardently championed the success stories of his own clinic, attributing these achievements to specialized strategies and a distinct approach that set his facility apart from others.

He then threw us a curveball: he wouldn't be able to monitor my progress remotely if we chose Denver. "Our infrastructure just isn't set up for that kind of collaboration," Dr. Crosse said with regret. It was a logistics challenge we hadn't seen coming. He further admonished us about the potential repercussions of my existing HHT condition, exacerbated by heightened estrogen levels and Denver's distinct altitude. These risks weren't trivial, encompassing dangers such as potential brain abscesses or even stroke. Pursuing this path would therefore necessitate temporarily relocating to Denver, an adjustment that would span roughly a month of fertility medication protocols.

By the session's end, Dr. Crosse's blend of professional assurance and seeming concern had made our decision to pursue Denver less definitive. But as we left his office, a nagging doubt remained. *Were his objections genuinely rooted in our best interests, or was there an underlying agenda to keep us tethered to his clinic?* The delicate balance between heartfelt advice and potential ulterior motives cast shadows on our path, leaving us more uncertain than ever.

So, with a heightened sense of anticipation laced with trepidation, we committed to another round of IVF in Toronto. This wasn't just another step—it felt like being on the edge of a precipice, knowing the depth of the fall but hoping for the beauty of flight. As Amy's drug regimen was about to commence, aiming for a January 2001 embryo transfer, Dr. Crosse, in a more personal moment, inquired if I'd be open to speaking with a few couples seeking guidance on surrogacy. Sharing the intricacies of my experience, with its ups and downs, became not only a therapeutic outlet but also a way to build bridges of understanding and camaraderie in a process often marred by isolation.

During the emotional ebbs and flows, we found a moment of peace in a much-needed family trip to Florida. The getaway was my attempt to put a little distance between myself and the relentless cycle of IVF treatments, to catch my breath. But life has a way of bringing you back to reality, even when you're trying to escape it. Strolling through a grocery store aisle, I was struck by the sight of a father laughing with his twin daughters. Their easy joy and close connection were a bittersweet reminder of what might have been for us. The impact was deeply felt, coming just days after I'd received the tissue report—a clinical confirmation of the identical twins we had lost, two girls. It was a tender, poignant moment that nudged my hidden sorrows back to the surface.

At times, I couldn't help but question whether our struggles to conceive were a sign that we weren't yet ready for another child. *Who really held the reins? Was it divine* intervention, medical expertise, or the fallible science we were so dependent on?

My emotions seemed caught in an unyielding tide, where hope clashed violently with despair, and optimism seemed constantly shadowed by fear. *Could I ever still the ceaseless whirlpool of thoughts, even for just a fleeting moment?*

January 19, 2001

> Day 7 of this IVF cycle finds me in an odd emotional limbo. The initial discomfort in my chest has faded, replaced by a strange calm. Amy's uterus is in "prime condition," says Dr. Crosse, and my own eggs are developing just as they should. We're aiming for an extraction by Wednesday or Thursday.
>
> While physically everything seems on track, emotionally I'm in uncharted territory. Amy's treatment regimen has changed; she's on different drugs designed to make her body more hospitable for the embryos. She'll also take blood thinners to ensure optimal uterine blood flow. It's reassuring, yet it raises unspoken questions—like why these steps weren't part of our earlier attempts. But I choose not to dwell on that; questioning the past won't change the present.
>
> When I first began this journal, its blank pages felt overwhelming, almost as if they were daring me to fill them with something meaningful. Now, I see that won't be a problem.

January 26, 2001

> Yesterday marked our pivotal egg retrieval day, and the results exceeded my expectations: out of the twenty eggs retrieved, a

promising sixteen have been fertilized successfully. The day began with us arriving at the clinic at 8 a.m. Once again, the procedure itself was not without discomfort. The intensity of the physical pain was remarkable, but my determination to have another baby eclipsed it, a vivid reminder of the intricate interplay between our physical and emotional selves. With sixteen viable candidates, I hope for a successful transfer on Sunday. Coincidentally, it's also the day of the Super Bowl. While the world places bets on their teams, I'm placing mine on a different kind of victory.

January 29, 2001

The air felt thick with possibility yesterday, the day of Amy's embryo transfer. Kenny and I had spent the preceding days huddled in whispered conversation, wrestling with a proposal from Dr. Crosse—four embryos, not just two or three. The term "selective reduction," a euphemism cloaked in clinical detachment, was reintroduced into our discussions. Dr. Crosse maintained that, if necessary, we could travel to Detroit, Michigan, just across our border, where a specialized clinic offered the procedure with an acclaimed "100% success rate," without harming the remaining fetus or fetuses. What did "success" truly mean in such a context?

We grappled with this ethical minefield, but our core aim remained unshaken—to welcome a healthy baby into the world. I didn't want to have to go on fertility meds again.

Amy, resolute and supportive, was with us every step of the way. She stood beside us, equally invested in the fragile potential of these embryos, whose quality, as declared by Dr.

Crosse, would guarantee "eight or nine cell divisions by day three." Those words shimmered with promise. We didn't put all our eggs in one basket—pun unintended. Eight other embryos were frozen, all representing suspended possibility.

With the transfer behind us, we find ourselves in a quiet limbo. Each moment stretches, filling with both hope and trepidation. It's a suspenseful stillness as we await the phone call that could forever alter the course of our lives.

Dearest Reader: Have you ever struggled to keep your relationships balanced while navigating pivotal moments in your life?

MILE 11

THE BALANCE OF RHYTHM

Hope is indeed a curious thing. Throughout my adult life, whenever I purchase a lottery ticket, I tuck it away in my wallet and forget about it, letting it linger there for months. The very act of not knowing whether I've won keeps me filled with optimism and hope, knowing there's a chance, however slim, of winning a significant sum of money. It's interesting how the absence of certainty can fuel our positivity and hopefulness. The unknown, whether in the realm of winning a lottery or achieving a successful pregnancy, allows that glimmer of hope to persist. There's something about not having a definite answer that leaves room for optimism to thrive. It may sound peculiar, but it resonates deeply within me. *Do you know what I mean?*

The clock had never seemed as intrusive as it did in those days leading up to Amy's official pregnancy test. Each tick amplified the unease settling in the pit of my stomach. Amy's recent bout of severe nausea had done little to calm our nerves. On that fateful day, she held a small plastic stick that promised either peace of mind or shattered dreams. It read negative. Before my panic could fully set in, Dr. Crosse was quick to remind us that over-the-counter tests weren't definitive.

At the time, I felt like I was on a relentless seesaw of optimism and dread. *Was Amy's unease simply a side effect from her medications, or could it be indicating that a new life was beginning to grow inside her?* Watching her struggle tore at me, magnifying the awe I already had for her bravery and commitment to my and Kenny's future.

Endless questions churned through my mind. *Should we shift our gaze to that Colorado clinic we had considered before? Could the use of frozen embryos be our answer?* Amy's symptoms were impossible to ignore, and her forthright confession only sunk me further into a sea of doubt. "If this doesn't work," she'd said with a voice steeped in exhaustion and sadness, "I think you'll have to find a new surrogate." Her words brought an unexpected burden I hadn't anticipated.

Heeding Dr. Crosse's advice, we chose to await the blood test results, which would deliver a more conclusive verdict in just a few days. Every second was tinged with both anticipation and worry.

February 11, 2001

As Sunday morning dawns, the air feels dense with a heaviness I can't shake. The negative result from Thursday's home pregnancy test haunts me, despite all my attempts to brace for whatever today might confirm. My heart is a clenched fist, each beat echoing the doubts and questions that have been plaguing me: How much more can our spirits bear? What financial and emotional tolls await us in this labyrinth of fertility?

The doctor's office is stark and sterile, a cold contrast to the tumult raging within me. Its foggy windows mirror my blurred state of mind. Amy stands beside me as she prepares for her blood test, and although she doesn't say much, her exhaustion is an unspoken weight we're both carrying. Returning home, I try to distract myself, but the wait for the phone call is torture.

Over the past nine months, Amy has faced an endless cycle of injections, hormone treatments, and emotional upheavals. Our tears have flowed freely, a testament to our shared struggle. We've endured four unsuccessful embryo transfers, including a devastating miscarriage culminating in a D&C procedure. Amy's resilience has been nothing short of heroic; I have no doubt she's given this pursuit every ounce of her strength.

When my phone finally rings at 2:37 p.m., I cross my fingers. As I answer, reality hits me like a ton of bricks.

We're not pregnant.

The grief comes crashing in on multiple fronts—the immediate sorrow of this moment, compounded by the daunting possibility of starting over with a different carrier. Each setback seems to push my dream further into the horizon, adding another layer to the already unbearable burden of sorrow.

Finding a rhythm when you run is much like maneuvering the convoluted paths of life. At first, every step feels heavy, filled with uncertainty and hesitation. It takes a conscious effort to synchronize your breath with your stride, to quiet the doubts that scream for your attention. But then, somewhere along the way, you reach a state of flow. You find a cadence that works just for you—a pace that pushes you but doesn't break you. Your breathing becomes your metronome, each inhalation and exhalation a reassurance that you're still moving. It's a subtle yet profound shift, from enduring to flowing. Establishing your pace doesn't make the challenges vanish, but it does turn them into bearable milestones. This harmony gives you focus and infuses each step with purpose, propelling you forward regardless of the hurdles in your way.

Surrogacy felt like walking through a maze without a map. From the fertility protocols to our doctor and our surrogate, nothing seemed to fit together in a way that felt right. This lack of balance left me disoriented. I couldn't find my rhythm.

Dearest Reader: Have you ever felt hopeful and hopeless at the same time?

MILE 12

EDUCATION VS. PERSUASION

Reflecting on that period of my life, I feel a mix of astonishment and self-criticism. How, as an educated woman, did I tread so deeply into the waters of surrogacy without grasping the full scientific and medical intricacies? It's all too common, isn't it? We often place implicit trust in those we view as experts without constantly pausing to critically analyze the path they're setting for us.

When I geared up for marathon training, I researched meticulously to understand the subtleties of nutrition, hydration, and training regimens. Knowing felt like an essential part of the process for me. Yet, with surrogacy, my approach was strikingly different. Driven by a fierce "whatever it takes" determination to expand our family, I didn't adequately equip myself with a holistic grasp of the fertility issues that affect conception, the embryological mechanisms, or the advancements in reproductive technology. It's only in retrospect that I see the importance of such foundational knowledge in guiding our decisions.

The vulnerability of those seeking fertility treatments cannot be overstated. Many, like me, are fueled by an unwavering desire to have a child. This earnestness can sometimes make them more malleable to skewed information or less transparent practices. The crux lies in education—knowing the nuances, the terminologies, the procedures. Such understanding enables patients to pose the right questions, to probe, and sometimes to challenge or seek additional perspectives.

In an industry without stringent regulations, there's a risk. Certain clinics, sensing the desperation, might sometimes amplify their success narratives or reframe data to project a rosier picture than reality. Their strategies could be built on persuasion, preying on hopes more than delivering genuine results.

My gullibility is obvious to me now. I ventured into this without a compass, and Kenny, trusting my lead, followed. Initially, we didn't pause to truly deconstruct our setbacks but rather clung to a sliver of hope that hinted at a successful outcome.

The dance between education and persuasion is intricate, especially in realms like fertility treatments. An informed individual, possessing the right knowledge, can both trust medical professionals and maintain a healthy skepticism. This balance ensures that the journey, while hopeful, remains grounded in reality. In recognizing the varied practices across fertility clinics, it's crucial to stay inquisitive for the best possible results.

In February 2001, we were introduced to another prospective gestational surrogate through the same agency that had connected us with Amy. Krista, a single mother and part-time nurse who lived about two hours from Toronto, immediately struck me with her down-to-earth personality during a few lengthy phone conversations. Our face-to-face meeting had to be postponed due to her upcoming vacation, but I felt both hopeful and wary about this new direction.

Hope, always a double-edged sword, felt particularly risky now. Alongside this, Kenny and I took a pragmatic step and scheduled a consultation with a social worker specializing in adoption. It seemed crucial to explore every avenue available, to consider every possible path.

Yet, a melancholy lingered as I investigated these new opportunities. Friends, family, and strangers peppered me with unending questions about family expansion, even asking about my ability to conceive again. Each question was a poke at a wound that only grew more raw. While I kept telling myself that this sadness would eventually subside, I also knew that the hole in my heart wasn't something that could be easily filled.

Upon Krista's return from her vacation, Kenny and I made the two-hour drive to meet her. My heart raced as we entered the restaurant; she was already there, waiting, and I recognized her instantly. Meeting her in person solidified my impression from our phone conversation—she was warm and delightful. We spoke about our families; she listened intently to our story and shared endearing tales about her seven-year-old daughter. By the meal's end, she voiced her willingness to assist us. I felt Kenny's subtle nudge under the table, a silent expression of excitement.

Afterwards, I updated Dr. Crosse about our potential surrogate, and he shared our happiness. We quickly arranged for her to undergo a thorough assessment at his clinic the subsequent week—this involved consultations with a psychologist and legal professionals to initiate the required documentation. Even though the waiting continued, it was tempered by the renewed hope brought on by partnering with a new surrogate.

As for adoption, we hired a social worker to conduct a home study, a mandated step in the procedure. Our interactions with the social worker were constructive, though the volume of paperwork and administrative hoops was staggering. We were tasked with gathering four reference letters to vouch for our suitability as adoptive parents—one from a relative and three from friends. Juggling all these commitments was admittedly draining. The weight of it all, combined with my deep longing for another child, left me feeling stretched thin and emotionally exposed.

On Hannah's second birthday, April 2, 2001, we had our preliminary meeting with Dr. Crosse. Krista drove into Toronto, and together we made our way downtown. An unexpected bright spot in the day was running into a familiar parking attendant. He recognized me and generously only charged $5 for parking, a kind gesture down from the usual $13. It's the small, unexpected acts of kindness that sometimes offer a soothing sense of normalcy and gratitude. Krista underwent the required tests without a hitch. Dr. Crosse had scheduled a uterine sonogram[1] after her upcoming period as the next step. We intended to use our frozen embryos. I teetered between hope and worry.

April 15, 2001

Today, the contract from our lawyer is finally ready to be handed over to Krista. As I scan through the pages one last

---

[1] A uterine sonogram (sonohysterography) is an imaging test that uses high-frequency sound waves to create pictures of the uterus and surrounding pelvic structures. It is commonly used for diagnosing abnormalities and monitoring pregnancy. Source: Johns Hopkins Medicine, Health: Treatments, Tests and Therapies, "Sonohysterography."

time, the legal jargon swims before my eyes, each clause and stipulation adding to the sense of gravity. Meanwhile, I've also been managing financial logistics. I canceled Amy's bank card and set up a new one for Krista, ensuring that she has the means to cover any expenses related to fertility and pregnancy from a designated account. Each of these tasks, however mundane, feels like another stone added to an already heavy load.

Witnessing friends joyously announce their second child is a kind of sweetness that's just out of my reach. And yet, Hannah never fails to punctuate my day with her laughter, each giggle a tangible reminder of the joys we've already cultivated. Kenny's constant support echoes through his calming voice, his reassuring touches, and his eyes that tell me, "Our turn is coming." But despite these moments of comfort and clarity, the ache of unfulfilled dreams persists. I find myself yearning for the day when the dense mist of longing and uncertainty finally lifts.

The transfer scheduled for that Saturday gave rise to a vortex of emotions difficult to put into words. Dr. Crosse provided a glimmer of optimism, stating that Krista's uterus appeared favorable for implantation. But then he complicated matters by suggesting we transfer six embryos in total, two of which didn't meet the highest quality standards. This recommendation was far from trivial; it added another layer to an already complex situation.

Meanwhile, Krista was facing delays with her legal paperwork, compelling me to connect her with a contact at our law firm to expedite the process.

For a better understanding, I circled back to Dr. Crosse to discuss the embryo count. He reiterated a point he'd made when Amy was our surrogate: implanting multiple embryos might create a supportive environment for successful implantation. The embryos that don't implant will disintegrate, providing essential nutrients to the ones that do establish themselves in the womb.

Despite this additional information, I still found myself in a quandary. Deciding on the number of embryos to implant extended beyond medical reasoning to touch on ethical considerations. I had to balance the promise of creating life with the substantial dangers posed to Krista, as well as to any children that might result. This became a complicated nexus of competing factors—each one a blend of hope, risk, and accountability—along with the potential for complications like multiple births.

April 21, 2001

The ink had barely dried on the contract when the moment arrived for the embryo transfer this morning. The procedure was smooth, buoying our spirits. Following Dr. Crosse's earlier advice—and based on our past experiences with Amy—we took the calculated gamble of implanting four viable embryos out of an initial six.

In the hushed atmosphere of the clinic, I found myself scanning the faces of five other women, each engrossed in her own world, each awaiting her own life-altering procedure. A thought wedged itself into my mind: statistics dictate that only one of us will likely emerge from this stage with a successful pregnancy. My heart aches for all of us to defy those odds, but a raw, unvarnished part of me yearns for this round to be ours. Now, we face a twelve-day wait, a stretch of time filled with cautious optimism and the weight of past disappointments.

April 28, 2001

A week has elapsed. During our most recent call, Krista described a lingering nausea and nighttime breast tenderness. Her voice wavered between hopefulness and hesitancy, vocalizing the tightrope we were all walking. My heart leans into the notion that she's pregnant, yet my mind counterbalances, reminding me of our previous five attempts. "Why should this round be any different?" it interjects skeptically. Almost daily, I find myself asking Kenny if he thinks this attempt will be the one that succeeds, much like a child on a long car ride repeatedly asking, "Are we there yet?" Each time, he encourages me to maintain faith.

Of late, dreams punctuate my sleep with enigmatic messages. In one vivid tableau, I see Krista holding up a pregnancy test to reveal a pink line. In others, ethereal infants come into view only to fade with the morning light. Whether these nocturnal visions are windows to my subconscious or mere amalgamations of my daily oscillation between hope and fear, they further deepen the emotional landscape of this experience.

May 14, 2001

Where do I even begin? The news of the negative test result lands like a sledgehammer to the chest. After a year, two surrogates, and a reservoir of hope drained dry, this defeat feels monumental.

Krista, too, is distraught, her body having mimicked pregnancy symptoms due to the medications she's been on.

Last week's consultation with Dr. Crosse unveiled new strategies and treatments. While these changes might offer some hope for the future, they have also ignited a spark of resentment within me. He has new strategies and new treatment plans as if the past attempts were just trial runs. Why is he only now suggesting a completely different approach? Why hadn't these changes been recommended for our previous fresh transfer with Amy? What adds salt to the wound is his recent contradiction. After assuring me that the frozen embryo transfer with Krista looked promising, he now backpedals, telling me those embryos were of only "middling quality."

As I wade through this tumult of emotion, I find symbolism in our next scheduled retrieval date, June 18. In Jewish tradition, the number 18 symbolizes "chai," which means life. At this moment, I'm open to any signs of hope or meaningful coincidence.

Today's clinic visit yielded more than hormonal stats and medical jargon. A chat with the in-house social worker shifted my perspective slightly. "This isn't a disaster, it's a hiccup," she offered, urging me to focus on the more promising fresh transfer ahead.

As our home study approaches its conclusion, the notion of adoption resurfaces—perhaps a less clinical road but just as fraught with emotional landmines. Yet, it might lead us to offer love to a child in need.

Answers are scarce, but what's clear is that this journey is stretching me in ways I never imagined. At times, I feel trapped in stasis while everyone else moves on. Today is a hard day to be positive.

On a sunlit May afternoon, while Hannah and I walked with a friend of mine and her two children, we crossed paths with a familiar face from our music class. Her unmistakably pregnant silhouette hinted at the imminent arrival of her second child. As she asked about Hannah's age, I sensed an unspoken question in her gaze, a silent inquiry, perhaps a judgment lurking in the backdrop. After the initial pleasantries, the conversation drifted to the benefits of having siblings close in age. "It's such an advantage when they're close in age, just like my two will be," she remarked. For a brief instant, my thoughts meandered back to the years of my own upbringing, a time resonant with laughter and shared secrets with my brother, a connection firmly rooted in the narrow years separating Adam and myself. However, recollections of my sister also emerged. Despite the wide ten-year gap between Aarin and me, our bond has remained strong and steadfast. Standing there, the weight of this woman's words pressed heavily, with envy and sorrow forming a knot in my throat. Underneath my effort to mask it, a deep-seated ache threatened to spill from my eyes. The casual chatter felt like a series of piercing jabs, each phrase a painful reminder of our ongoing struggles to give Hannah a sibling. Trying to shield my vulnerability, I focused on my daughter, pretending to be preoccupied with her ice cream that threatened to melt away, much like my composure.

Facing another round of IVF felt like climbing a mountain all over again. Each step, heavy with anticipation and hope, was accompanied by a nagging uncertainty that whispered, *What if it doesn't work out this time?* The fear was real, palpable. Considering the what-ifs became a daily ritual. Thoughts of seeking treatment in the U.S. continued to float around—*but where would we even start?*

Around the same time, progress emerged on a different front. We wrapped up our home study for the adoption process. Awaiting us was the next step: drafting a heartfelt letter to a potential birth mother. Words, usually my refuge, now felt inadequate. *How do you encapsulate years of longing, hope, and dreams into a few paragraphs?*

Though I was well-versed in the rigors of long-distance running, grappling with surrogacy felt like cutting a path through uncharted territory, far removed from any race I'd ever known. There were no clear markers to guide the way, no cheering crowds to uplift the spirit, and no definite finish line in sight.

The thought of abandoning a vision I'd carried for so long—of expanding our family—was formidable, to say the least. It's challenging to face the prospect that a dream, nurtured and held close to the heart for years, might never materialize. However, contemplating this potential reality also compelled me to recognize the unquantifiable richness that Hannah had brought into our lives. If it turned out that she would be our only child, it wouldn't diminish her incredible worth or the love I had for her in any way. I knew that, while it would be a painful adjustment, I would gather the courage to accept this new trajectory.

Each day seemed to stretch into an endless loop of jealousy, frustration, and despair. But even during my lowest moments, a resilient voice within me would not be silenced, insisting, *This will not define you.* Struggling with these feelings, I reached for that reserve of inner strength I knew I had. Whatever lay ahead, I was prepared to confront it, fortified by both hope and unyielding determination. I reminded myself, time and again, that I was capable of weathering this storm because, deep down, I knew *I can do hard things.*

However arduous this journey, it began to reveal a different kind of truth. I started to see that maybe these hardships and challenges were shaping me in ways that would greatly influence who I am. *What if this journey wasn't a detour but a path to discovering a facet of my strength I never knew existed?*

May 25, 2001

Last night, I dreamt again. In this vision, my twin boys lay serenely in their swings, appearing only days, perhaps weeks, old. One sported a crown of dark hair, while the other mirrored my brother's fairer features. Their beauty filled my dreamscape with elation.

June 6, 2001

The ritual of Lupron shots has become second nature, a constant reminder of the path we tread, woven seamlessly into the fabric of my daily life. We stand on the cusp of our sixth IVF attempt, and with each passing day, anxiety and anticipation conduct a complex symphony within me. Today, Dr. Crosse presented a novel proposition: we only pay his fees if we succeed in achieving pregnancy. An unexpected relief mixed with trepidation. It's generous, but I can't shake the feeling: Is this a testament to his belief in us or a mere gamble?

Krista has committed to caffeine abstinence during this crucial time—a small but meaningful act that underscores her dedication. It's such actions that encapsulate the collective commitment we've made.

In a recent discussion with our surrogacy lawyer, I was drawn into a comparison between top-tier U.S. fertility clinics and the Canadian approach I've grown accustomed to. Kenny and I deliberately decided to stick with Toronto for this IVF cycle, a choice tinged with questions and reflective pauses. Was our decision to stay in familiar territory actually a comfort trap?

Amid these musings, my mother shared a narrative that snapped me out of my reverie. She told me of a couple who, after numerous disappointments with their initial surrogate, found success with another. Their triumph on their very first IVF cycle with this new carrier rekindled my sense of optimism. Later, as the couple and I engaged in an emotional hour-long conversation, I committed myself: once we reach our goal, I, too, will be a source of encouragement and wisdom for others facing similar challenges.

The Gonal-F[2] shots, a fertility medication used for inducing ovulation, were also now a regular part of my daily routine. I wouldn't say I had become an expert in administering them, but with two doses a day, I was certainly polishing my skills. I was holding up fairly well, albeit with an undercurrent of stress about the ticking clock, as we were keenly awaiting news of Krista commencing her menstrual cycle, which signaled the onset of her fertility medication regimen.

Krista and I had back-to-back appointments at the clinic, turning the morning into a relay of medical consultations. During the visit, Dr. Crosse once again reassured me about the excellent condition of my eggs, a consistent observation throughout. Yet, with each repetition of this assurance, a small part of me began to harbor doubts, wondering if his words were as promising as they sounded.

This growing skepticism crept into my interactions with the rest of the clinic staff. The constant self-monitoring—ensuring that my tone, choice of words, and timing were all just right—weighed on me profoundly. Moreover, the staff's discourteous behavior, which had been amplifying over time, only aggravated the situation. The dance of diplomacy with nurses, doctors, and receptionists was exhausting.

Even though Krista felt her period was imminent, and the blood work supported that feeling, it stubbornly remained out of reach. The sense that this cycle could slip away grew more acute, and the specter of past letdowns cast a shadow.

---

[2] Gonal-F, also known as follitropin alfa, is a synthetic version of the naturally occurring follicle-stimulating hormone (FSH). It is used as a fertility medication to help stimulate the development of eggs in the ovaries. Source: Drugs.com, "Gonal-F."

Kenny, however, remained optimistic. A scan revealed that an ovarian cyst was potentially causing the delay. Swiftly, Dr. Crosse recommended Krista start initiating progesterone injections.[3] We were informed that the cyst wouldn't hinder the embryo transfer.

On a day that seemed to encapsulate the unpredictability of our surrogacy journey, Krista was met with the challenge of an overbooked train, forcing her to contemplate a two-hour car ride with an aching back. The morning sun had barely risen when she rang me, a trace of worry in her voice. In the faint early light, I quickly plotted a route for her while driving to the doctor's office myself. After meeting at the downtown clinic, we drove back to my house, thinking she could catch a break before her drive home. But while trying to get everything right, we both had overlooked her blood work. Without missing a beat, we were back on the road, making our way to the clinic again. All this back and forth, while stressful, highlighted just how crucial every step of this process was.

As the echoes of that day's hectic pace began to wane, I found myself reflecting on the invisible chorus of support that had accompanied us thus far: from our immediate family to the fertility experts, legal advisers, and the kindhearted couples who had shared their own experiences with surrogacy. Even from the considerate parking attendant who frequently saw my early morning dashes and chose generosity over protocol.

---

[3] Progesterone injections for IVF are used to prepare the uterus for embryo implantation and to support early pregnancy maintenance. They are a key component during the luteal phase, the period between ovulation and embryo implantation, to ensure the endometrium is receptive for the embryo. Source: Elite IVF Clinic, "Progesterone Side Effects IVF: What to Expect?"

In that tranquil moment, I grasped that our tale wasn't solely ours. It was a quilt of collective hope and tenacity, woven from countless threads of understanding, skill, and camaraderie, each one pushing us closer to our dream.

Dearest Reader: In your experience, how do you manage the balance between optimism and skepticism when confronted with situations beyond your control?

MILE 13

AT THE CROSSROADS

As before, the absence of anesthesia left me acutely aware of every pinch and tug, resonating through me like a tango of hope and agony. Lying there, enduring each tactile sensation, the same thought that had accompanied me during past procedures made its way back into my consciousness: *This will be worth it.*

Dr. Crosse, whose manner often straddled the line between confident and arrogant, had pulled off what seemed like a small miracle. He'd managed to extract an impressive thirty-five eggs. "I'd say today was quite successful," he remarked, a smile touching the corners of his mouth, though his eyes remained inscrutable.

The sun hadn't fully risen, and I was already entangled in a whirlwind of emotions. The call from Dr. Crosse came in when I least expected it. "We have a remarkable number: twenty-seven of the thirty-five eggs have successfully fertilized," he said, sounding almost smug. The following day, the number had shifted to twenty-four. "The transfer is tomorrow," I murmured, a silent prayer escaping my lips, hoping the universe would work in our favor.

By 8:15 a.m., we were at the clinic. The anticipation made every minute feel like an hour. When we finally entered the procedure room around 9:30 a.m., I felt an unexpected calm.

That was until Dr. Crosse began discussing the embryos' progress. His demeanor had shifted. The confident doctor was now replaced by one burdened with delivering unsettling news. From the promising twenty-four, we were now down to ten viable embryos. The room seemed to shrink.

Dr. Crosse delved into the specifics: the eight-cell embryos, the six-cell ones, all the way down to those that had only reached the two- and four-cell stages. His voice faded out as I tried to process the situation. Suddenly, he dropped a bombshell. "I recommend we transfer all ten viable embryos," he said, his tone urgent. The burden of that suggestion was immense, and the number felt overwhelming. There was an air of nonchalance about him when again he raised the prospect of selective reduction if more than two embryos were implanted successfully. The potential complications seemed to be merely a footnote in his proposed course of action. His focus was clear: maximize the chances of conception.

His explanations about the lab's performance and my egg quality started to meld into an indistinct murmur as my focus faltered. A persistent thought echoed in my mind: *Conceiving Hannah had been a seamless experience, so why was this journey so fraught with challenges? Could the fertility treatments have thrown things off balance, or was there another underlying issue?* Yet, Dr. Crosse's unwavering assurance influenced our decision.

Reflecting on it now, I'm acutely aware of the ethical quandary surrounding the transfer of ten embryos. Yet, in that moment, Dr. Crosse's certainty and seeming expertise painted a different picture. He strongly advocated that this approach was our best opportunity. Krista, too, was convinced. Drawn in by his confidence, we were both willing to clutch at any strand of hope. In hindsight, it's clear that Dr. Crosse's desperation mirrored our own.

A few days passed, and Krista reported classic signs of pregnancy: consistent nausea, a heightened sense of smell, and overwhelming fatigue. We dared to hope. Yet, every pregnancy test she took mercilessly showed a negative result. The anguish of heartache had become a bitter companion. Even with the shadow of doubt, I clung to the possibility that the blood test would reveal a different outcome. But as the week drew to a close, my fears were confirmed—she wasn't pregnant.

Three hundred and sixty-nine days since our miscarriage, we seemed stuck in the same agonizing spot with no discernible progress. As I ushered in my thirties, the silent wishes I cast upon my birthday candles felt suspended in the ether, unrealized. Time, in its unfaltering pace, doesn't pause for personal heartaches. That same week, Krista faced a harrowing experience. She began her period and unexpectedly expelled her entire uterine lining. Severe cramps marked the onset, and she passed what resembled a sac. I had suspected a miscarriage, but medical evaluations indicated it was her lining.

Dr. Crosse offered no ground-breaking insights as to why this attempt didn't succeed, casually suggesting egg donation as an option. Faced with this proposition, we were more inclined toward adoption than venturing into the uncertain territory of using a donor egg. I remained steadfast in my belief that my eggs were still viable. The science, the very reasoning behind it, should have been on our side. There might have been a flaw in their procedure or a limitation in their lab techniques. It was time to seek advice where trust in science coexisted with empathy and understanding. I was becoming increasingly doubtful that Dr. Crosse could offer us that balance. When asked about future plans if we chose to undergo another IVF attempt with him, he referred us to a colleague in California, Dr. Matthew David. I was already familiar with Dr. David, having read his book. Dr. Crosse also mentioned potential adjustments to our drug regimen. His sudden recommendation for a U.S. clinic, after previously advising against it, raised questions about his consistency and undermined our trust in his judgment.

With the clarity that time brings, I often look back at my younger self's decisions with a wince. As you follow this narrative, you might find yourself asking the question I've grappled with countless times: *Why did she continue to place her trust in Dr. Crosse?* Each time I asked this of myself, it was with a sharp pang of self-reproach. My apprehensions about the financial implications of seeking treatment in the U.S. might have anchored me to Dr. Crosse, but hindsight highlights the folly of that decision. *How blind can the heart be when it's driven by hope and desperation?*

Our conversation with Dr. David on July 31, 2001, was illuminating. He stressed perseverance and introduced an entirely different drug protocol, which even Dr. Crosse believed could be transformative.

On a different yet equally important note, we met with the adoption social worker. The next steps involved creating a profile, a window into our lives for potential birth parents. While the path of adoption shimmered with promise, it also presented its unique hurdles. The widespread concept of "open adoption" pressed on my heart, making the idea of continual communication with the birth parents feel somewhat invasive. The silent looming fear of potential future rejection from an adopted child would occasionally arise too. My heart also wrestled with society's impulse to label children as "adopted." *Why must there be a need to attach such qualifiers to one's relationship?* The term *adopted* shouldn't define or overshadow the depth and purity of a bond.

<u>August 8, 2001</u>

> As I sit on the deck of the family cottage, a warm cup of coffee nestled in my hands, a gentle mist waltzes across the surface of the lake. A chipmunk darts along the picnic table, its tiny feet a brief patter. The rising sun begins to pierce the early morning veil, promising a day of new beginnings.
>
> Once again, the retreat up north has been my sanctuary, shielding me from the omnipresent sights of expectant mothers and newborns—a momentary reprieve.
>
> With the home study behind us, my attention has shifted to the vast landscape of domestic and international adoption agencies. Exploring these choices provokes both optimism and anxiety.
>
> Lately, I wrestle with a haunting question: Is this journey a form of punishment, or could it be a concealed gift? As I reflect, I think of Hannah, who arrived ahead of her time and, in doing so, became the catalyst that saved my life. Her early arrival alerted me to my HHT, a hidden danger lurking within, averting the risk of a stroke or brain abscess. From this perspective, it doesn't feel like punishment but rather a fortuitous turn of events. Watching Hannah

flourish day by day fills my heart with an overwhelming sense of gratitude.

Last night, my period began, heralding the start of a new cycle. As the first day unfolds, we stand at the outset once more, ready to travel down this familiar path.

After my consultation with Dr. Crosse, I started a dual medication regimen to optimize conditions for successful egg retrieval. For two weeks I was on birth control pills to regulate my menstrual cycle while also taking Metformin[1] to balance my hormone levels.

Adjusting to my new routine of pills and injections was like a balancing act—careful, precarious, but doable. Then Krista called, her voice not its usual anchor of assurance but a tremble of doubt that made my footing wobble. "I've been doing a lot of soul-searching," she said. Her words carried a hesitancy that felt like the thick electric air before a storm—loaded, imminent. "I'm reconsidering continuing this cycle."

An icy knot of dread tightened in my gut. The idea of halting this attempt halfway through, especially after the regimen of medications I'd begun, sent a shockwave of panic through me. Bridging the fragile silence, I picked each word with painstaking care, fully aware that she held the power to either fortify or shatter what we'd started. "Krista," I began, striving to thread empathy and urgency into my tone, "if this cycle succeeds, you'll be committed to carrying my child for the next nine months. We need unshakable unity for that."

---

[1] Metformin helps regulate menstrual cycles, reduce insulin and androgen levels, and may improve the chances of pregnancy. Source: Nova IVF Fertility, "What is Metformin and why it is used in fertility treatment?"

After a moment's pause, she replied, "And that is precisely why I don't want to move forward anymore. I thought I could do this, but now I'm not so sure."

I ended the call, my emotions still churning. Needing further insight, I hesitated momentarily before picking up the phone again. My fingers finally dialed Mary, the lynchpin who had connected us with Krista. As she spoke, her words filled the room—offering both a glimmer of understanding and a lens through which to view Krista's sudden hesitation. She mentioned Krista's taxing weekend and the nausea the medications had triggered. At that moment, I couldn't help but wonder, *Had we rushed back into another IVF cycle too quickly?* My patience wore gossamer-thin; every tick of the clock felt like an eternity.

Mary's voice, tinged with realism and a subtle trace of hope, hinted that Krista might still recommit. If not, the daunting task of finding a new surrogate loomed—a monumental challenge given the scant number of available gestational carriers and the growing list of waiting couples.

Our attorney's recommendation lingered in the air, like a challenging crossroads ahead. A specialist in New Jersey could be our next step, a path fraught with emotional, physical, and financial complexities we hadn't yet fully considered. As we stood at this formidable junction, it became increasingly clear that change was our only viable option.

In my training for the marathon, there were moments of sheer exhilaration, runs where I felt invincible, as if I could continue forever. But not all runs are equal. Some days brought invisible hurdles that demanded recalibration. Around the 10-mile (16 km) mark during one session, an unwelcome sensation invaded my right knee. No adjustments to my stride or gait seemed to alleviate the nagging discomfort. As if in solidarity, my left knee soon joined in, forcing me to equip both knees with supportive sleeves. It was as though my body was signaling the need for a tactical shift.

It was frustrating to experience this setback in my regimen, but little did I know that a simple visit to a store specializing in all things running would provide the key to addressing the root cause of my knee pain. I entered the store wanting to buy a pair of quality running socks. I engaged in a conversation with the knowledgeable salesperson about my training and the challenges I was facing. Surprisingly, they suggested that my shoes might be contributing to the discomfort. The idea hadn't occurred to me before, but I was intrigued by the possibility. With their guidance, I tried on a pair of shoes that boasted advanced foam padding designed to absorb the impact of each step. Curiosity got the better of me, and I decided to put them to the test on my treadmill at home. The difference was immediate and astounding. The new shoes provided the support and cushioning needed to alleviate the strain on my knees. It became evident that my shoes had been the underlying issue, sabotaging my training progress.

This realization hit me hard. It was a valuable lesson relearned—the importance of addressing the root cause rather than settling for temporary solutions. My mind couldn't help but draw parallels with our arduous IVF journey under Dr. Crosse. Consumed with the desire for a successful pregnancy for almost two years, I had neglected to investigate the underlying factors contributing to our failures. These weren't just abstract concepts but tangible variables—different fertility protocols, the cocktail of fertility medications, and the expertise at embryology labs. All these elements had been overshadowed as I narrowly focused on the end goal of pregnancy.

It's only when we dive into the core issue that we can redirect our path toward genuine, enduring progress.

Even though I still wore the sleeves as a precaution, the shoes transformed my running experience. They not only relieved my knee pain but also restored my confidence in pursuing my training goals. That simple outing for socks led me to a solution I didn't even know I needed.

Like those transformative shoes, the solutions to our challenges often materialize from unanticipated directions. I suppose it's all part of the learning process, reminding me that the path to achieving our heartfelt desires is rarely a straight line. It took me a couple of years to fully grasp the impact of making changes on our surrogacy journey.

When Krista chose to break our agreement, my world felt like it was disintegrating. Fully cognizant of the difficulties she was managing, I extended various offers to ease her burden—from housecleaning to gardening. But despite my earnest attempts, she refused each offer.

Faced with Krista's sudden change of heart, Kenny and I found ourselves on shaky ground, standing at a difficult intersection. One road led to the devil we knew: the Toronto clinic, where despite seven unsuccessful attempts, the routines and protocols were familiar. The other road ventured into the unknown intricacies of American healthcare. However, after numerous sleepless nights filled with serious discussions, we started to see things more clearly. Setting our sights on the U.S., we solidified our commitment. And for the first time in a long while, a sense of possibility illuminated our path ahead. After thorough research, we chose a top-tier clinic in New Jersey, known for its cutting-edge expertise and compassionate care in reproductive medicine.

Heading to the United States for treatment was not without its considerations. Beyond the substantial financial investment, we knew we would have less direct involvement with an American gestational carrier. Nevertheless, we were willing to trade familiarity for a chance at success, motivated by the advanced options the New Jersey clinic had to offer.

September 2, 2001

As I pen the final lines of this journal, the complexities of surrogacy continue to reveal themselves.

Eighteen months have passed in a blur since embarking on our IVF odyssey, yet each day's impact has carved itself indelibly into my being. Time has played dual roles: as both a relentless bandit stealing moments and as a sage imparting hard-earned lessons. The road has been arduous and sometimes agonizing, but I have faith that these experiences will one day shimmer with meaning. Concurrently, our aspirations for adoption are gradually coming to life. Our family dossier is complete, and with the fall season on the horizon, we're gearing up for a mandatory adoption seminar—a critical juncture toward earning a spot on the agency's list of prospective parents.

As I turn from the last page of this journal to the fresh pages of another, I visualize a narrative brimming with hope and the fulfillment of our surrogacy endeavor. The love from Kenny and Hannah reminds me that even in my loneliest moments, I'm never truly alone. The strength of my parents lifts me, unspoken but always present. And while Adam and Aarin may not grasp every nuance of our quest, their earnest care is a balm.

My spirit is raw but ignited, ready to etch tales of dreams pursued and mountains moved.

Dearest Reader: How have you grappled with pursuing your dreams while braving the intricate challenges of your journey?

PART III

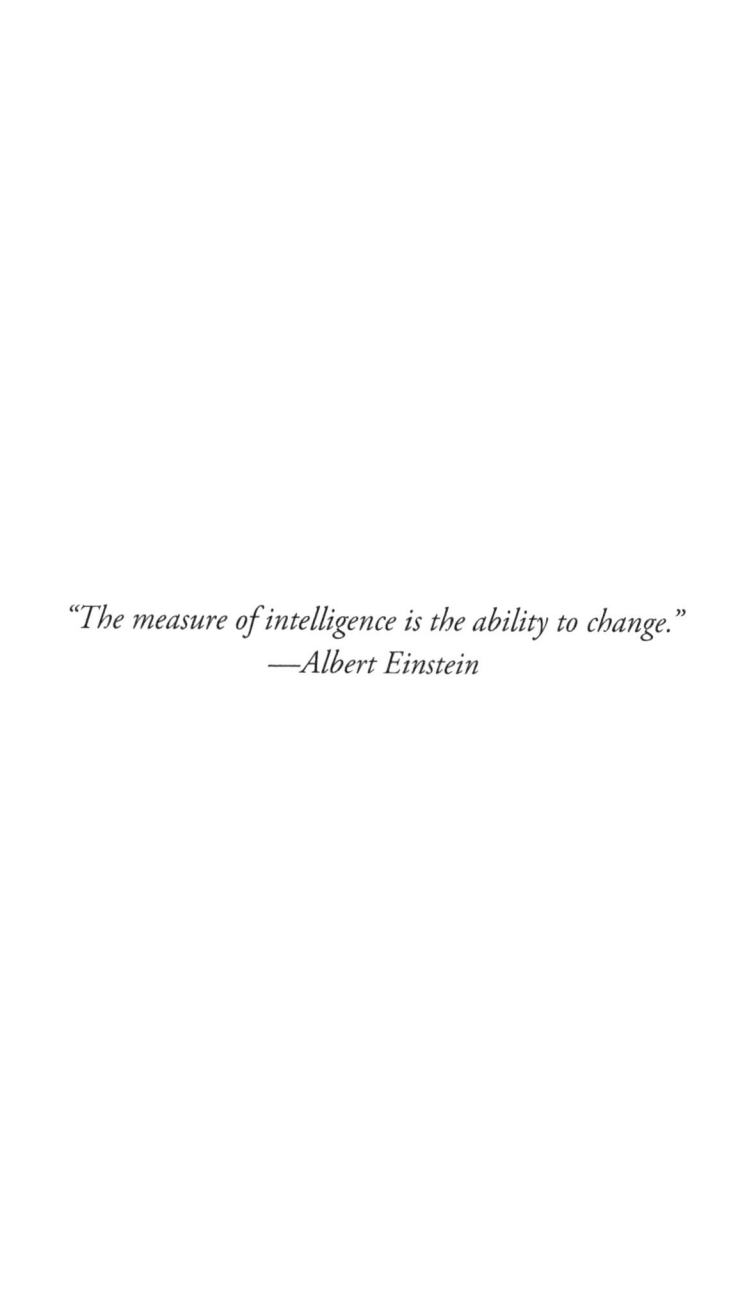

"The measure of intelligence is the ability to change."
—*Albert Einstein*

MILE 14

WELCOME TO THE U.S.A.

Kenny and I plunged back into surrogacy but were blindsided by the financial demands we would eventually face. Our savings, once robust, had thinned out considerably by the time we encountered the sky-high expenses inherent to U.S. surrogacy. Yet, we had something not everyone had—a family ready and willing to extend a financial lifeline. Swallowing our pride to ask felt like admitting defeat, but what a luxury it was to even have such an option. Their backing wasn't just financial relief; it was a stark reminder of our fortunate circumstance in a dream where money couldn't create happiness but could facilitate its pursuit.

Kenny's initial hesitation to accept help began to waver when he was met with such unconditional support. This wasn't charity; it was a collective family effort, shouldering both dreams and burdens together. The realization that we were not alone on this tumultuous path was a comfort few are afforded.

Society often cloaks the act of seeking help in shame, labeling it as a weakness rather than as an embodiment of strength and cooperation. This notion was distinctly contradicted during my marathon experience. The spirit of unity and camaraderie displayed among the participants was uplifting. Runners faltering from various hurdles were not isolated but aided by others—be it fellow participants, volunteers, or spectators. This spirit of assistance pervaded the event, from helping a stumbling runner regain footing to a concerned volunteer ensuring my well-being as I stretched post-race. These gestures emphasized the innate human tendency to assist one another.

Draining our life savings for the hope of a larger family was a choice laden with consequences that continue to ripple into our everyday lives. Yet, buoyed by the support of loved ones—a privilege we never took for granted—I would make the same choice again without hesitation.

About a week after 9/11, Kenny and I embarked on a pivotal road trip to Morristown, New Jersey. There, we met Melissa Brisman, an attorney who matched intended parents with gestational surrogates. Melissa exuded understanding, sharing personal anecdotes from her own surrogacy experience. This not only lent depth to our meetings but created a sense of solidarity and shared journey. We had encountered this phenomenon before. Both Mary and the infertility specialist back in Toronto had also brought their personal experiences with surrogacy and infertility into their professional realms.

Entering the Assisted Fertility Specialists (AFS) clinic in Morristown, we felt an immediate sense of hope. The thoughtful design and soft lighting offered a warm contrast to the artificial atmosphere of the Toronto clinic.

As Dr. Derek Marshall extended his hand, his demeanor radiated a blend of youthful energy and seasoned expertise. We followed him into his office, and he pored over our medical history and prior experiences. It felt as though we were beginning a new, more hopeful chapter. Looking up from our file, he assured us, "Given your age and the fact that you've successfully conceived a healthy child before, I don't foresee any major fertility hurdles ahead for you."

While Morristown represented new beginnings for us, the remnants of September 11 in New York City were ever-present. At one point along our route, from the car we could see the sight of distant dust and lingering smoke. This haunting reminder made our personal journey feel both intimate and dwarfed. The shared sorrow in the community was tangible. *In the shadow of such monumental loss, how do you hold on to personal ambitions when the world around you is so deeply steeped in grief?*

To manage costs, we decided to do some of our preliminary testing in Toronto. Dr. Crosse, once hesitant, now seemed more flexible, adapting clinic protocols to accommodate us. I was never sure about the reason behind his change of mind. *Maybe he knew he hadn't lived up to his earlier assurances?*

Meanwhile, at home, dismantling Hannah's crib was a moment fraught with emotions. It was a milestone, for sure—her transition to a "Big Girl" bed—but it was hard to shake off a sense of loss. Yet, ever pragmatic, Kenny nudged me to focus on a future where we'd reassemble it for another baby.

As we browsed through the various profiles of potential gestational carriers that Melissa had presented, Sherry's stood out. She was a married mother of four from Pennsylvania, and on paper she seemed like a good choice (even though I couldn't help but wonder how well one could really gauge suitability from a profile). Her parenting background was a positive factor, but the real confirmation as an ideal match remained to be determined. Eager but cautious, we scheduled a phone call, wondering if this could be the connection that would propel us forward.

This promising lead coincided with another celebrated milestone—our fifth wedding anniversary. As Kenny and I paused to reflect over the past five years, we marveled at the unexpected twists and turns life had taken us on. Hannah's early arrival, my medical challenges, and our ongoing efforts to expand our family were all far from what we'd imagined on our wedding day. Yet, despite these hurdles, our relationship had only become stronger.

October 15, 2001

> *They often say "Good things come to those who wait." I embrace this adage, but there are moments when the gravity of delay becomes overwhelming. I envision a future where our children read these words, feeling the depth of our desire to have them with us. Each day brings us closer to that dream, even when the journey's end seems elusive.*
>
> *Amid new mothers pushing double strollers and expectant women glowing with anticipation, I sometimes let my thoughts wander. What if I tried to conceive again, taking every possible precaution to mitigate the risks? This fleeting idea visits me often, but deep within, I recognize the potential consequences for Hannah and Kenny. The very presence of these thoughts underscores the intricacies of our path.*

I remember feeling drained from the formal and somewhat stiff introductory call with Melissa and Sherry, where we raised some sensitive topics. Melissa's voice echoed through the phone: "Let's touch upon some crucial aspects.

What are your viewpoints on matters like abortion or selective reduction?" We had a candid exchange, sharing our opinions openly and honestly. Sherry was also emphatic that the pregnancy would be ours, assuring that any decisions about it would rest solely with us. Despite the weight of the conversation, there was a sense of accomplishment by the end of it. Kenny and I thought the initial discussion went well, and Melissa echoed our positive sentiments, telling us that Sherry was keen to proceed. While I couldn't help but feel a sense of excitement, I remained cautious and reserved. We still had a long and uncertain road ahead.

A few days later, I took the initiative and reached out to Sherry directly, setting the stage for our collaboration. I felt a mix of anticipation and anxiety about speaking to her and her husband, Frank, hoping to bridge the gap between us. From the outset, Frank's demeanor was unexpected. He interrupted Sherry a few times and at one point remarked, "She might be doing this out of the kindness of her heart, but I'm looking forward to a new flat-screen." Even though he laughed it off, the comment lingered in the air, adding a layer of unease to our conversation. Sherry quickly tried to smooth over the awkwardness, saying, with a dismissive chuckle, "Oh, that's just Frank being Frank, always the joker. Don't mind him." Despite Sherry's attempt to lighten the mood, Frank's words had already left an indelible impression. The rest of the discussion was a precarious balance. Their carefree manner sharply contrasted with my vulnerability, bubbling up from my deep-seated wish for everything to fall into place smoothly.

Then Sherry brought up a scheduling hiccup. We had initially hoped for a November appointment at AFS, but

Sherry had run out of vacation days at work and needed to push it to January. While this was far from ideal, especially with the psychological consult in the balance, we were left with little choice. Melissa stepped in to offer perspective. Searching for a new carrier could lead us to the same timeline or even longer, she pointed out. With Sherry, we at least had the advantage of completing most of the preliminary requirements beforehand, such as blood work and background checks. Melissa was responsible for initiating these screenings once a carrier was matched with intended parents. The major delays would revolve around the ultrasound and psychological consultation at AFS. Despite these affirmations, I was haunted by the possibility of Sherry having second thoughts or becoming unsuitable due to unforeseen complications. More daunting, however, was the thought of starting from scratch again, with all its time and emotional implications.

As the conversation progressed, Sherry's voice took on a hint of vulnerability. "My biggest worry," she began hesitantly, "is that you won't be able to make it in time for the delivery. I really want you both there with me."

I could sense the depth of her sentiment and quickly reassured her, "Sherry, I promise you nothing will keep me from being in that delivery room."

Her candid fear took me back to the early stages of my surrogacy exploration. I'd learned that many gestational carriers embark on this path filled with optimism, largely because their personal experiences with fertility had been unproblematic. The possibility of setbacks, complications, or failures didn't cross their minds. While some might consider this naive, to me it represented a rare form of hope—untainted by life's typical disappointments and skepticism. I clung to it.

Reflecting on our exchange, I realized I was straddling a delicate line between hope and guardedness. Unlike my previous experiences, I wasn't leaning strongly toward optimism or pessimism. I was simply present, taking things day by day. Perhaps it was a lesson that life intended to teach me: the most rewarding things aren't easily achieved. Hannah's birth itself stood as a vivid testament to that truth.

In the rhythm of my long-distance runs, I've learned a mantra: *Take things one step at a time, address each challenge as it comes, and always move forward.* On difficult stretches, my mind frequently tempts me with the idea of stopping or slowing down. But just as I push through in my runs, re-evaluating with every stride, life often mirrors this interplay between challenge and perseverance.

One such test of certitude came when trying to contact Sherry. When I was informed that her number had been disconnected, a simple call became complicated. The immediate fears—*Had she changed her mind? Was she distancing herself from us?*—raced through my mind. However, after a frantic call to our lawyer, I learned that her phone line was temporarily down. Just a small hurdle, not unlike those momentary doubts on a run. But it made me ponder future challenges: *Might there be times when Sherry is hard to reach?*

Once we got back in touch, our conversation naturally turned to the upcoming medical procedures and our scheduled visit to AFS on January 17, 2002. Anticipating a transfer in late February or early March, we now had a milestone to aim for.

In my weekly conversations with Sherry, I often felt I carried most of the dialogue. The warmth and camaraderie I'd experienced with previous carriers seemed missing, making our talks feel more transactional than personal. When I asked about her family, her replies were consistently brief, usually limited to a simple "Nothing much is happening on our end." She was often a closed door, offering little insight into her life or feelings. Yet, there were times when she expressed sincere enthusiasm for our shared journey. Those moments provided a flicker of connection, but I couldn't help but sense a lingering emotional distance. I repeatedly emphasized that my communication was driven by a genuine desire to know her and her family on a deeper level, but it often felt like an uphill battle. My running mantra echoed in the background. Every step forward, though small, was significant.

November 18, 2001

Yesterday, Sherry, her husband, and I were engaged in a conversation filled with mutual understanding. Sherry spoke of her personal progress, reflecting her dedication to caring for her body in preparation for the upcoming transfer. With only two months before we meet at AFS to begin her mock cycle[1]—a practice run to optimize hormonal conditions for the actual IVF—an unmistakable sense of expectation stirs within me, coupled with a strong belief that we're on the road to success.

Often, I find myself lost in thoughts of the future, perhaps a year ahead, maybe greeting a new life. Anxiety and

---

[1] An IVF mock cycle, also known as a mock embryo transfer cycle, is a simulation of the procedure without the actual transfer of embryos. It replicates various steps of a regular embryo transfer cycle, such as preparing the uterine lining and evaluating the uterine cavity. Source: Progyny, "Understanding the Purpose and Benefits of an IVF Mock Cycle."

exhilaration course through me. I anticipate a time when I'll reflect on these moments, grasping the true essence of patience and seeing order in what feels like disarray right now. I often tell others that life has its way of aligning the stars, even when the design eludes us. The challenge is not just to say it but to truly believe it.

When the day comes that I hold my next child, every second will be held in reverence, no moment overlooked.

That entry was written more than two decades ago, and its sentiment still resonates within me. The odyssey of parenthood demands an unparalleled combination of resilience, patience, and ceaseless energy. Amid sleepless nights and constant worries, it has shaped and taxed me in ways I couldn't have imagined. The profound essence of becoming a parent has never been lost on me. It has imbued my life with abundant joys, sorrows, victories, and lessons, immeasurably enriching my existence. And for that, my heart swells with endless gratitude.

Dearest Reader: Have you ever hesitated to ask for help? Has that affected your life and choices?

MILE 15

TIMELINES AND LANDMINES

In the biting cold of December 2001, Kenny and I once again stepped into the all-too-familiar corridors of our old fertility clinic. Dr. Crosse's presence did little to warm the atmosphere. His pride seemingly wounded, he remarked, "Considering what you're spending in New Jersey, you could have received the same services here for less." Suppressing my rising irritation, I retorted, "We entrusted you with seven tries, but sadly, none led to success." He briefly met my gaze, a flash of annoyance evident, then turned away without another word. Though tempted to voice my frustrations further, I reminded myself of our primary objective: initial monitoring and obtaining the necessary fertility medications, not engaging in his ego battles.

December 31, 2001

It's New Year's Eve, and I've been enjoying our family holiday in Florida. There's something ineffable in the air: a mingling of hope, excitement, and reflection. Amid the laughter and beachside antics, emotional moments sneak up on me, threatening to spill over. Tonight's celebration transcends the simple changing of date; it's a rekindling, a quiet acknowledgment that the year ahead will bring us nearer to the fulfillment we've been striving for.

Hannah, at only two, possesses a depth in her gaze, as if she's seen eons beyond her years. Her laughter grounds me, even in the stormiest moments. Driven by an unyielding curiosity, she seems intent on exploring the intricate architecture of the world. When it comes to her empathy, she soaks up the feelings around her, mirroring a breadth of understanding that leaves me marveling. In Hannah, I find a wellspring of love and renewal.

Sherry and Frank have been preparing diligently. Both have undergone the necessary blood tests to ensure that neither of them have transmissible diseases that could affect a pregnancy, a vital precaution due to their sexual relationship. In addition, Sherry visited her OB today to set things in motion for her mock cycle. My chats with Gillian, the registered nurse at AFS overseeing the surrogacy program, have become more frequent and detailed, marking our progress. Together, we're targeting the start of my drug protocol for March, with the hopeful anticipation of welcoming a December baby. Their diligent actions and our collaborative planning reinforce the deep commitment we all share for the journey ahead, nurturing a sense of realistic expectation. Yet, beneath our careful optimism, I am conscious that even the most meticulously laid-out strategy isn't immune to unforeseen challenges.

Continued delays caused a thick fog of tension to settle, growing denser each day to cloud my thoughts. When Sherry's uterine sonogram got postponed, our carefully crafted plans seemed to be absorbed into this mist. With medical results still in limbo and legal discussions about background checks adding more layers of uncertainty, my confidence was tested yet again.

I tried to pierce through this haze during a phone conversation with Sherry. Laced with urgency, my voice underscored the need to keep moving forward. Feeling the weight of my words, she promptly rescheduled her sonogram to January 17 at AFS. The news brought relief and clarity; it felt like we had regained our footing.

Just as things started to become more straightforward, another twist along our path appeared. A call from Melissa's agency, specifically from the background checker, carried an undertone that pricked at my senses. The revelation: Frank, Sherry's husband, was ensnared in an extended background check due to past legal tangles. I was told that his results would be available in a few weeks. My heart, which had just begun to find its rhythm, stumbled again. I asked Melissa to dig deeper, cautious to shield Sherry and Frank from my burgeoning concerns. The findings offered comfort but with a hint of disquiet: supposedly, Frank's review had resulted from youthful indiscretions. Though not a roadblock, the news carried with it a distant rumble of thunder, too far away to worry about yet but close enough to remind you that clear skies don't last forever.

Sherry's health and well-being were essential for the upcoming transfer and the duration of the pregnancy. Frank's support was also key. A week separated us from meeting them in New Jersey. Prudent optimism filled me as the countdown began, each passing day bringing us closer to a defining moment.

On Wednesday, January 16, 2002, Sherry and Frank checked into the hotel. The phone's ring, signaling their arrival, had Kenny and me pausing for a moment, our eyes locking in anticipation and apprehension. We headed down to the agreed-upon meeting spot outside the hotel's restaurant, my footsteps quick but measured, as if keeping pace with my pounding heart. There she stood, Sherry, just as she'd appeared in the photos we'd scrutinized for weeks. She wore a floral dress that clung modestly to her figure, and her hair carried the subtle scent of lavender. Frank was beside her, a bit shorter than I'd imagined, in a simple button-down shirt and slacks.

As we settled into our seats for dinner, the mood was ambivalent. Clinking silverware and murmuring diners provided a backdrop, yet it was the subtle dynamics between Sherry and Frank that held my focus. Tiny telling details—the slight narrowing of Sherry's eyes, the relentless tap of Frank's foot beneath the table—suggested a tension, unspoken yet impossible to ignore.

"Everything's set for the initial procedures," Sherry offered, her delivery sounding calculated, as if she'd rehearsed the line.

"Good to hear," I responded, my voice strained and my smile a facade as I absentmindedly pushed around the food on my plate.

"We're eager to get this underway," Frank chimed in, his hesitant tone mirroring my internal unease. Under the table, I reached for Kenny's hand, gripping it for reassurance.

By the time dessert was served—a cheesecake that seemed to lack any taste, likely due to my heightened state—I couldn't shake the nagging feeling that something was amiss. While their words conveyed assurance, their body language spoke of a story not yet fully revealed. As we parted ways on that indelible January evening, I couldn't escape the feeling that this was merely the prologue to a difficult narrative yet to unfold.

Kenny and I returned to our hotel room in silence, each lost in our own thoughts about our experience at dinner. He couldn't help but notice something was off too. Sensing my distress, he embraced me, gently suggesting, "Let's focus on tomorrow and see how things play out at the clinic." He paused before adding reassuringly, "Any concerns we have, we can address then." As he rubbed my back to soothe my nerves, I said, "Okay," finding comfort in his calming presence, as always.

Thursday morning began on a more hopeful note. The uterine sonogram had cleared Sherry of any complications. Kenny and I had our session with the psychologist, and we felt things were moving smoothly. We left the room for Sherry and Frank to have their consultation. We sat down in the waiting area, flipping through magazines. As time seemed to drag on, my uneasy feeling crept back in.

I glanced at the wall clock—it ticked louder and louder in my ears, like a drumbeat.

"Something's not right," I said to Kenny, the words barely more than a whisper.

"Should you knock on the door?" he replied. "We're cutting it close with our flight."

"I think I have to," I said, standing up, my stomach tangled with nerves. Just as my hand was about to make contact with the door, it swung open. The psychologist appeared, and one look at her face told us something was very wrong. She closed the door behind her and motioned for us to step aside.

"I'm afraid there's something you need to know," she began, her voice filled with regret. "Sherry has a history of drug addiction, twelve years, although she has been clean for the past six. Frank has his own bag of legal issues, and—most concerning—there are questions about the stability of their relationship."

The floor seemed to drop away from me. It was a gut-wrenching moment, as if reality had twisted itself into a terrible, unrecognizable shape. The betrayal hit me like a tidal wave, leaving me struggling for air. Turning to Kenny, I saw his expression reflecting my own shock, a look of disbelief and devastation washing over him just as intensely. Fighting to keep my composure, I informed Sherry and Frank that we needed time to process everything. The atmosphere was tense, Sherry's apologetic demeanor contrasting with Frank's anger. Sherry, in a strained attempt at reassurance, said, "It's been ages since I last used drugs. I assure you, I wouldn't risk anything if I were to carry your baby." The real struggle for me, however, was more internal—a turbulent mix of deception, disappointment, and dread.

In a state of emotional upheaval, Kenny and I got into a taxi bound for Newark Airport. My hands shook uncontrollably as I dialed Melissa's number. "Melissa, it's unraveling—all of it..." I choked out. Each word was saturated with desperate anguish. It felt like life had taken a baseball bat and swung it mercilessly at my knees. The line was silent, the air heavy with anticipation. Melissa's voice eventually broke through, marked by concern. "I... I can't believe this," she managed to say. "I'll call AFS and uncover what happened. But right now, it's important you know I'm committed to finding you another gestational carrier," she declared, the resolve unmistakable in her voice. Despite her confidence, my mind was ensnared by the six months we had lost. Kenny and I held hands, silently acknowledging the weight of our situation as we traveled toward the airport.

We made it to our flight by the skin of our teeth, rushing through the terminal as if trying to outpace the turmoil inside us. The moment the plane ascended, the barriers crumbled and my tears streamed uncontrollably—I could no longer contain the shattered hope and surging anger. I just wanted to be back home in Toronto, to find comfort in hugging Hannah.

The following day, Melissa called. Her voice alone, heavy with gravity, hinted at further bad news. "There's more," she began. "I just got Frank's criminal record. It's extensive, going back years."

Her revelation struck hard, dismantling what little trust I had managed to hold on to. Frozen in disbelief, I tried to absorb the enormity of their deceit. "Melissa, how did this slip through? Aren't criminal background checks standard before introducing carriers to intended parents?"

Melissa's response was tinged with regret. "Alison, she wasn't truthful. She omitted key details on her intake form and misled my assistant during her initial interview about her drug history and Frank's criminal record." There was also an apologetic note in her voice, perhaps a realization that their past should have been scrutinized more thoroughly from the start.

Then Melissa shared something that hit even harder. "Sherry didn't want her past to define her," she relayed. That statement felt like a cruel irony. It seemed Sherry was so consumed by her narrative of redemption that she failed to consider the impact of her half-truths on others' lives.

For a moment, I was speechless. "Why?" I finally exhaled, sorrow and indignation in my voice. "Why is this happening to us?"

Melissa paused, perhaps searching for words that could offer some form of comfort, but what could she say? "I'm so sorry," she replied softly.

What cut me the deepest was the loss of time—irrecoverable, irredeemable time. "Time is all we've really lost," Kenny said, trying to comfort me. But it wasn't just time. The financial toll was undeniable too—the expenses for flights, hotels, and their preliminary medical tests, all seemingly wasted. Kenny offered another way to look at it: perhaps this was a form of divine intervention, sparing us from a more complicated future with a surrogate and her spouse mired in deceit. Though I wanted to take solace in that, the notion only provided a glimmer of comfort. Time was not just a series of moments slipping away; it was a reservoir for my hope, a hope that was both my anchor and my Achilles heel.

So I pondered: *Where did this relentless optimism come from? Was it just naïveté, or was it a divine gift? Could it be sheer human resilience?* I wished I'd had clear answers. Insights alluded me. All I knew was that this persistent hope was a double-edged sword. It was what made every setback painfully devastating but also what empowered me to rise again, to dry my tears, to confront the future, to be in the arena. It pushed me onward, urging me to replace the disheartened question of *Why me?* with a defiant *Why not me?* as I ventured once more into the uncertain void ahead. In that maelstrom of conflicting thoughts and feelings, I came face to face with the intricate paradox of hope—a force with the dual capacity to wound deeply, yet also to heal.

Later that same afternoon, Melissa introduced us to Laura, a surrogate who lived in Florida. She was in the midst of carrying twins for another couple but expressed enthusiasm about embarking on a new surrogacy partnership with us following their birth. I didn't know what to feel. *Hopeful?*

<u>February 3, 2002</u>

I've gone back to therapy, a step that's provided me with an indispensable, impartial lens through which to process my current life circumstances. My therapist doesn't just offer a shoulder to lean on; she challenges me to break the cycle of suspended living. One practical suggestion she's given is for me to engage in a hobby, an outlet to channel my energies and distract from the singular focus on having another child. The point is clear: living for tomorrow's hypotheticals robs today of its vitality. When the time comes to adapt to another child, we'll handle it. But for now, my life shouldn't be a reel of paused frames awaiting that moment.

I emailed our previous surrogate, Sherry, and her husband, Frank, thanking them for their initial willingness to help us expand our family. The message was more for my own sense of closure than for any expected reply. When they didn't respond, it didn't sting. Given their past duplicity, their silence was both anticipated and inconsequential. I've come to terms with it, which has only strengthened my conviction to move forward.

Running has always served me as both exercise and a form of therapy. During this time, I found a mental clarity that was often elusive elsewhere. Each mile offered not just a release of endorphins but also a sense of progress. Nature, too, became a silent partner in this emotional pilgrimage, its scenic trails and open skies serving as a backdrop to my internal monologue. It provided a connection with a universe larger than my immediate troubles. Every source of strength and clarity, whether it came from therapy or my early morning runs, was not just welcomed; it was essential.

Dearest Reader: What is your strategy to restore trust in yourself, others, and the journey you're on?

MILE 16

ON THE CUSP

We decided to go ahead with Laura, the carrier Melissa had introduced us to in January, who was on the cusp of giving birth to twins for another couple. Our timeline was contingent on her receiving medical clearance to conceive again. The doctors estimated that it would be around eight weeks after she delivered the twins. We penciled in our initial meeting in New Jersey at AFS for May 6.

Choosing Laura came with its own set of costs—literally. Experienced carriers tend to be more expensive. But what we paid in dollars, we gained in certainty. Laura knew the ropes and understood the challenges and nuances of the surrogacy process, being a mother to three children and in the midst of her second surrogacy arrangement. Partnering with us would mark her third time as a surrogate. Melissa was optimistic too, confident that Laura's body would bounce back quickly, as it had after her previous pregnancies.

So there we were, back in a familiar state of pause, a holding pattern that was becoming all too routine for us. This time, however, the waiting was softened by a small but meaningful assurance: we were waiting for a carrier who, at least, had a proven track record. It was far from a certainty, but it was something.

Progress on the adoption front had slowed, and our social worker informed us that it could be a year or two before we received any updates. Given this delay and our existing priorities, we decided to pause our adoption efforts. Instead, we chose to focus on supporting our current surrogate.

March 30, 2002

Now, well over two years into this surrogacy journey, I find myself still suspended in a strange blend of hope and uncertainty. As Hannah approaches her third birthday, every day accentuates the relentless pace of time. I typically keep in regular touch with Laura, but her silence over the past week has been unsettling. My thoughts drift to the calendar, and with every unanswered call, the chances of a June embryo transfer seem to diminish.

In the midst of this agonizing wait, I've found a semblance of refuge. Heeding my therapist's advice, I channeled my anxious energy into something tactile and tangible: designing lampshades. My fingers find comfort in the textures of repurposed fabrics: the smoothness of silk used in shade coverings, the softness of ribbons, and the delicate touch of handcrafted flowers fashioned from organza, felt, and chiffon. I've dubbed myself "The Shady Lady" —a lighthearted jest—but the act of creating these unique children's lamps has offered small moments of joy amid the prevailing unknown. Can you believe it? Who would've thought I'd go from losing sleep over my future to becoming the Vivienne Westwood of lampshades? If you told me a year ago that I'd be selling children's lamps in the midst of this whirlwind, I'd have thought you were joking! But hey, here I am, just trying to keep the lights on—literally!

However, the respite is often fleeting. Some days aren't about overcoming. Today, the weight of waiting feels like chains dragging me deeper into desolation. Unfulfilled dreams loom, casting long, unyielding shadows over my thoughts. I rise, I run, but each step feels more leaden than the last. I push forward, not because it's easy, but out of sheer necessity. Every moment of this endless waiting gnaws at my willpower. The burden of hope is sometimes the heaviest to bear.

I received the call from Laura's husband, explaining she had delivered the twins, and it was clear the birth had not been easy. He mentioned complications like toxemia[1] and issues with her uterine wall, his understanding limited by medical terminology. While grateful that the twins were healthy, a lingering concern for Laura's well-being filled me with unease.

Days later, another call from Laura brought unsettling news. Unaddressed complications from the earlier birth of her son compounded with the twins' birth had damaged her rectal muscles, requiring two surgeries and postponing any pregnancy plans for at least a year. The ground beneath me turned to quicksand as we faced yet another delay.

In the wake of this ceaseless string of setbacks, the thought crept in, insidious and tempting: *Perhaps it was time to give*

---

[1] Toxemia, also known as preeclampsia, is a pregnancy complication characterized by high blood pressure, proteinuria, and sometimes fluid retention and swelling, posing risks to both the mother and baby. Source: The American College of Obstetricians and Gynecologists, FAQs, "Preeclampsia and High Blood Pressure During Pregnancy."

up. I teetered on the edge of resignation. The fatigue of our unfulfilled quest began to pull me into a pit of bitterness. On impulse, I laced up my running shoes and set out, as if to outrun the creeping tendrils of despair.

As I pounded the pavement, my thoughts meandered to the concept of "hitting the wall" in long-distance running. It's that agonizing moment when you come face to face with your own limitations, where your muscles scream and your energy reserves are all but depleted. You find yourself at a mental and physical crossroads, grappling with whether to forge ahead or capitulate to the overwhelming urge to stop.

In that instant, the parallel struck me. My life had been like an endurance race, fraught with its own version of walls to overcome. Those walls—whether they had been failed IVF attempts, unforeseen medical complications, or emotional exhaustion—had been part and parcel of the journey toward expanding our family. But just as in any marathon, the race wasn't over until the finish line was crossed. While I acknowledged that walls existed in running as well as in life, I also recognized the power of resilience and determination. Yes, the barriers might have seemed insurmountable at times, but the walls were there to be scaled, circumvented, dismantled, or bridged. It hadn't been easy, but then again, nothing worthwhile ever was. With each stride back toward home, my resolve solidified: I would not let bitterness win; I wouldn't be consumed by what could have been or what was yet to come. Instead, I chose to continue running—both literally and metaphorically—toward the life and family I yearned for.

I first reached out to Melissa with an update that Laura would not be able to move forward as our surrogate. Soon after, I reconnected with Mary from the Ontario agency, hoping she might know of an available gestational carrier. It wasn't long before each had news to share.

On May 2, 2002, two possibilities unfolded, almost synchronously. Mary suggested a new candidate from Hamilton, Ontario, who was ready to start immediately. And Melissa's team had pinpointed Maureen from Pennsylvania, a young mother of two who worked as a phlebotomist and was eager to engage in this experience with us.

Speaking to Maureen over the phone was a breath of fresh air. She was a bundle of humble nerves, her voice trembling with the importance of the life-changing decision she was considering. The Ontario candidate was no less genuine, albeit candid about her financial motivations. She had reservations about working with a New Jersey clinic, yet she appeared receptive to the idea.

It was surreal to suddenly find myself with options where previously there had been none. I arranged another call with Melissa and Maureen and included her partner, Jeff, to ensure we all shared a common understanding. Additionally, I consulted Dr. Marshall from AFS in New Jersey for medical insights regarding the two candidates. He confirmed that both women were viable choices. However, he pointed out that the candidate from Ontario had already undergone her uterine sonogram and living closer would allow us a more hands-on experience throughout the pregnancy.

But as always, the unexpected had a way of shaping our journey. Just as I braced myself for a challenging decision, the Ontario candidate stepped back, citing medical concerns. It seemed as though destiny was guiding us, narrowing our options to one fated path.

Our follow-up conversation with Maureen amplified a fragile hope I'd been nurturing. She had already taken the steps to arrange all her necessary medical tests, a sign that she was as deeply invested in this undertaking as we were. It wasn't luck, perhaps, but for the first time in a while, I let myself feel something akin to it—a momentary exhale, releasing a breath I'd been holding for so long.

And so Kenny and I found ourselves, once again, boarding a plane, armed with a compilation of completed medical checks and tests, our emotions a swirl of apprehension and excitement. Although caution still tinged my optimism, another element was present this time. *Could this be the moment where long-standing hope intersects with real opportunity?* Maureen marked a positive shift. Her proactive and organized nature, even as I steered the process, introduced a level of partnership and support that was new and reassuring. The comprehensive background checks on both Maureen and Jeff, all clear, bolstered my trust, and highlighted Melissa's thorough vetting. For the first time in what felt like forever, our elusive goal seemed within reach.

Dearest Reader: *What pivotal moments have you faced when you were on the cusp of a significant change in your life, and how did you surmount those challenges to move forward?*

MILE 17

THE SURREAL IS REAL

<u>May 6, 2002</u>

Today was an extraordinary day! When was the last time I said that? Despite a rocky start, thanks to turbulence-induced nausea that left me doubled over a plane toilet, the day exceeded my every hope. We touched down in New Jersey and arrived at our hotel by 4:30 p.m., giving me enough time to freshen up and shake off the queasiness.

The hotel phone rang, jolting me from my thoughts as I sat on the edge of the bed.

"We're here," Maureen announced cheerfully on the other end of the line. My heart did a quick little dance; this was another critical juncture for us. Kenny and I went down to the lobby, where the air-conditioning made my skin prickle with goosebumps.

I spotted Maureen right away. She wore a flowy dress that echoed her gentle spirit. Her long hair framed a face adorned with a modest smile, her eyes twinkling with a mixture of excitement and shyness. Beside her stood her partner, Jeff, whose more subdued disposition perfectly complemented her natural presence.

The Surreal Is Real

"You must be Maureen! And Jeff?" I extended my hand. My voice full of a delight I couldn't contain: I was so relieved that it had bubbled up organically.

"Yes, it's so great to meet you, finally!" Maureen beamed, her eyes meeting mine in a moment of shared understanding. I felt an instant, tangible connection with her. Jeff exuded a reassuring calmness, his presence both comforting and kind. Exchanging a knowing look with Kenny, we both felt a sense of certainty that this was the right path forward.

Dinner felt less like a first meeting and more like a reunion with old friends. The restaurant hummed with the clatter of dishes and a soft, jazzy tune as we got to know one another. I felt a unity, a communal sense of purpose that had often eluded us before.

After dinner, we took a stroll through the quiet streets of Morristown. The night lights cast a soothing glow on the sidewalks, lending an intimate atmosphere to our walk. The air was scented with recently blossomed flowers, harmonizing with the lingering warmth of a late-spring evening. Our conversation was easy and free, every exchanged word and shared laugh building a sense of anticipation and camaraderie.

Back at the hotel, we played some pool. The clicks and clacks of the cue ball colliding with the others punctuated our discussion. Every shot we took—hits and misses alike—seemed to mirror the ups and downs of our fertility journey. And when the final ball found its pocket, a realization struck me: The line between us being hopeful strangers and dedicated teammates had been irrevocably crossed.

The next morning, we found ourselves back in a consultation room at AFS. The air was suffused with a clinical scent that barely concealed our simmering emotions. Maureen, sitting beside me, looked as if she was absorbing every word, every detail. This wasn't just a medical briefing; it was the blueprint for conceiving our next child.

Following this, we braced ourselves for the psychological assessment. Our psychologist, a familiar face on this emotional rollercoaster, welcomed us into her office. The atmosphere was charged with the unspoken words of our previous failure—a betrayal that had overshadowed our last visit. Kenny and I spoke earnestly, and when we left the room for Maureen and Jeff's individual assessment, the weight of history pressed upon us. We took a walk outside the clinic, as if trying to shake off the ghosts of our past.

Upon our return, the psychologist greeted us with a thumbs up, and the heavy air lifted immediately. "Everything looks great," she assured us. My eyes brimmed with tears; the room was suddenly brighter and warmer, as if illuminated by our collective relief. As we wrapped up our consultation, a sense of partnership engulfed us. "Thank you for doing this, for giving us hope," I said to Maureen, my voice charged with emotion. She nodded, eyes shimmering with the same feeling that had overwhelmed me.

As I sit in the terminal, waiting for the plane to take us back to Hannah, a profound sense of forward momentum sweeps through me, gradually displacing the uncertainties that have clouded my mind. The challenges ahead are still present, but for now they've stepped back, making room for this moment of progress and promise. Today has provided me not just relief but an invigorating sense of purpose, filling me with the energy to embrace whatever comes next.

Learning to let go has been one of the hardest lessons on this emotional rollercoaster. Every detail, no matter how small, felt like a monumental event with far-reaching consequences. Maureen's periodic retreats to her trailer, situated in a rustic, secluded campground, brought this challenge to the forefront. The silence, devoid of text updates or phone calls, exposed just how vulnerable I was in this intricate ballet of hormones and hopes.

The starting line was May 16, 2002: me with my birth control pills and Maureen with her Lupron injections. My dependency on Dr. Crosse's clinic for early monitoring soon surfaced as a bottleneck. Even after three pointed phone reminders, they lagged in sending over the critical blood work to AFS. Then, during one appointment, Dr. Crosse felt the need to critique my drug protocol: "Antagon[1] doesn't have the best reputation in Europe, you know." The words were soaked in irony—this was the same man who had once recommended the drug for our treatment. I bit my tongue but couldn't help thinking, *What a hypocrite.*

---

[1] Antagon (also known as ganirelix) is a medication commonly used in fertility treatments to prevent premature ovulation, thereby allowing for better timing and success of procedures such as IVF. It works by blocking the action of certain hormones in the body. Source: Drugs.com, "Antagon (Subcutaneous)."

Then came a nerve-racking hiccup: Maureen forgot her Estrace[2] tablets on a weekend at her trailer. An ultrasound revealed her uterine lining wasn't as robust as we'd hoped. Cue an urgent chat with Gillian, the nurse at AFS, who in her calming tone assured us, "Don't worry just yet. These readings are likely due to the missed medication. Let's wait for the next scan before sounding the alarms." Sure enough, the next ultrasound put us back on track.

From there, things started looking up. Maureen's mock cycle was nothing short of fantastic. As for myself, I embarked on an entirely distinct medication plan compared to my previous experience at the Toronto fertility clinic.

Kenny and I drove out to New Jersey, where AFS would oversee my cycle monitoring. The plan was for Kenny to leave the car with me and fly back to be with Hannah, only to return just before the egg retrieval procedure. And let's not forget his sacrificial task, performed "single-handedly," in service of this medical process!

I settled into my two-week stay in New Jersey, my spirits lifted by Dr. Marshall's encouraging update that my eggs were developing very well.

I quipped, "Well, I've done my part. Now it's your turn to deliver," pun intended. He laughed, then told me that they'd handle everything from here on out.

On July 2, the morning of my thirty-first birthday, Maureen came to Morristown to spend quality time with

---

[2] Estrace, a form of the female hormone estrogen, is commonly used in hormone replacement therapy. It is often prescribed for conditions such as menopause symptoms, osteoporosis prevention, and sometimes in fertility treatments to prepare the uterine lining for embryo implantation. Source: Drugs.com, "Estrace."

me. We shared a lovely lunch, followed by a leisurely walk downtown while attending to some errands. There was a distinct level of trust between us, a mutual respect that assured me of her ability to care deeply for the new life we were striving to bring into the world.

Not a single day passed without hearing Hannah's voice—it became a vital comfort, a soothing routine amid the chaos. Her photos were the first and last things I saw each day, placed lovingly on my nightstand. And thanks to Kenny, a gallery of short videos waited on my computer, each clip a valued keepsake that made the distance between us a little easier to bear.

For me? I became a cheerleader for my eggs. Just like I'd coax myself to keep running on those tougher days— *You've got this; dig deep*—I believed my eggs deserved their own boost of inspiration. It was like reminding myself of my resilience as a runner; I needed them to know they'd be in good hands once Maureen took over. The goal was a successful retrieval, and, mirroring my approach to running, my guiding principle remained *One step at a time.*

July 10, 2002

We'd managed to retrieve eighteen eggs, shattering the average count of eight to ten that I'd been told to expect. Today, we're all but holding our collective breath, awaiting the news of how many were successfully fertilized.

The egg retrieval under Dr. Marshall's guidance was a stark contrast to my experience in Toronto. While some soreness lingered afterwards, it was far less severe than the intense discomfort I had previously endured. Thanks to the anesthesia, I felt no discomfort during the procedure itself. Throughout our time in New Jersey, Dr. Marshall has been an unwavering source of support, prioritizing my well-being and ensuring Kenny and I were both informed and comfortably cared for.

And then, the call we had all been waiting for. Of the eighteen eggs, thirteen had fertilized. We were looking at potential transfer days—either Friday, Sunday, or Monday. We will know definitively by Friday morning. One milestone at a time, we keep moving forward.

<u>July 12, 2002</u>

The long-awaited transfer day finally arrived, and it unfolded more smoothly than I could have imagined. The day began with an 8:30 a.m. call from Maureen, informing us that the clinic had advised her to arrive between 11 and 11:30 a.m. Sleep had eluded me the previous night due to a whirlpool of excitement and anxiety. To add to the stress, a fire drill at 5:30 a.m. had us evacuating the hotel. I hoped tonight would be free from such disruptions; Maureen and Jeff were staying at the same hotel, and she needed her rest.

Seeking some semblance of peace, I called the clinic to inquire about our embryos' status. They deferred, stating that the details would come during the transfer. Anxiety mounting yet again, I attempted to center myself. We were at the clinic by 11 a.m. Once there, Maureen began hydrating—necessary for the ultrasound-guided catheter placement. Clad in scrubs, we were ready to go.

The Surreal Is Real

Once in the procedure room, Dr. Marshall announced that we had three viable embryos. Instantly, my mind raced to the remaining ten, but he assuaged my fears: eight were still under development. Our three embryos looked great, he reported. A promising sign that brought tears to my eyes. Kenny gently squeezed my hand.

Transferring more than three embryos would risk high-order multiples, the doctor explained, a scenario he deemed unethical. This was another far contrast from the guidance we'd received from Dr. Crosse. The ten-minute procedure was seamless, and we watched on a television monitor as the three embryos traveled through the catheter and into our surrogate's uterus. Following a twenty-minute rest, Maureen retreated to our hotel. Off work until the following Thursday, she'll undergo an hCG/blood pregnancy test on July 23. Now, we are in a ten-day waiting period, during which I remain cautiously optimistic for a successful outcome.

Tomorrow morning, we head home. I can hardly wait to see Hannah; it feels surreal to have come this far. The journey continues—one day, one hope, one possibility at a time. Sticky thoughts abound!

As the ten days were nearing their end, Kenny and I were on the road, returning from a wedding in Ottawa, Ontario. Rain tapped incessantly against the windshield, each drop echoing the tension that knotted my stomach. Kenny glanced at me, understanding in his eyes. "Call Maureen, if it will help ease your mind," he encouraged softly.

What I really wanted was for Maureen to take a home pregnancy test, so I dialed Gillian, our nurse at AFS, unsure if I was seeking her opinion or simply her blessing. Her words of caution against a urine test tightened the knot of anxiety in my stomach. "However," she said, "an earlier blood test could be an option." That offered me a small sense of agency amid my swirling thoughts. Hanging up, I immediately rang Maureen. Knowing she was at work and a phlebotomist, I asked if she could arrange for a colleague to administer the blood test.

"I'll see who's available in the lab today," she replied.

"Let me know as soon as you do," I said, not even trying to hide the urgency in my voice.

As time passed, my mute phone amplified my dread. *Why hasn't she called yet?* I stared at the device as if I could will it to ring. I couldn't take it any longer. I called Maureen again.

"I'm with a patient. Can you call back in ten minutes?"

Time crawled. Each second felt like its own minute, each minute an hour. Kenny tried to calm the storm inside me. "If it's good news, she'll want to savor the moment," he reasoned. But his soothing words couldn't dispel my worries.

At last, I redialed Maureen's number. "Switch me to speakerphone," she instructed. The rain outside seemed to pound against the car roof in sync with my heightened heartbeat—each drop a tiny drumroll leading up to something monumental. Just then, as if the universe was interjecting into this charged moment, a car zipped past us. The licence plate caught my eye, leaving me momentarily stunned: "TRIPLETS." Whether a cosmic joke, a tantalizing clue, or a sign of auspicious things to come, it vanished as quickly as it appeared, swallowed by the rain-soaked road ahead.

I found myself holding my breath, the air around me suddenly electric with anticipation—as if lighting were about to strike. And then Maureen said the words that had eluded me for nearly thirty-six agonizing months: "We're pregnant."

Overwhelmed, Kenny and I found ourselves instantly shedding tears. The burden of so much time filled with hope, frustration, and countless what-ifs seemed to lift off our shoulders in that ineffable moment. Years of holding our breath had culminated in a relief so profound that neither of us could conceal it.

Gillian's subsequent phone call, imbued with jubilant tones, soon followed. She speculated that the elevated hCG levels might be indicative of twins. The unfolding reality felt almost too perfect, almost too fragile. Though ecstatic, I was also terrified that something could go wrong.

Could we dare to believe? My heart was soaring and sinking simultaneously, caught in a tangle of exhilaration and terror. Memories of past disappointments lingered, muting my joy with caution. I was elated, yes, but also paralyzed by the daunting thought of life's unpredictability, of how happiness can sometimes be snatched away without warning.

Maureen called me from the doctor's office after our first ultrasound. Two sacs had appeared on the screen—TWINS! She seemed increasingly well, and while my heart expanded with a newfound excitement, a corner of my mind whispered that we weren't out of the woods yet.

We passed the six-week mark, reaching halfway through the critical first trimester. Was this long-held dream finally about to materialize? Would we actually be blessed with not one, but three children? Each day felt like a fragile step on a tightrope walk between immense hope and lingering apprehension.

Our parents were overjoyed when we told them, but we decided to keep the pregnancy a closely guarded secret from everyone else for the time being. Despite myself, though, I couldn't resist sharing the news with my brother and sister.

In running, there are days when everything just clicks. You feel invigorated throughout the run, and even at the end, you're brimming with energy, as though you could keep going. You're strong, healthy, and empowered. Yet, you know the importance of restraint—meeting your goal for the day and stopping there. Pushing too hard risks injury, and you want to be able to run again tomorrow. That's how I was feeling in that moment. Strong and empowered, yes, but cautious not to let my emotions get ahead of me. We were still at the initial stages of this process, and it was essential to keep a realistic perspective.

Dearest Reader: How do you reconcile moments where profound hope intertwines with the echoes of past pain?

MILE 18

THE COMPLEXITY OF CREATION

Everything seemed to be progressing smoothly—until it wasn't. The phone rang, and Maureen's voice on the other end was shaky. "I'm so sorry," she said. At eleven weeks gestation, she had just undergone a nuchal translucency ultrasound,[1] a relatively new and noninvasive procedure that measures the fluid at the back of a baby's neck to assess the risk of chromosomal abnormalities. The ultrasound had revealed a cystic hygroma[2]—a fluid-filled sac at the back of Baby B's neck—that put us on a collision course with a 75% chance of chromosomal abnormalities. The next step? An amniocentesis[3] for both babies, which is a test where a small amount of

---

[1] A nuchal translucency (NT) ultrasound is a first-trimester pregnancy screening that measures the amount of fluid behind the baby's neck to assess the risk of chromosomal abnormalities. Source: The Cleveland Clinic's Health Library, Diagnostics & Testing, "Nuchal Translucency."
[2] A cystic hygroma, also known as lymphangioma, is a birth defect manifesting as a sac-like structure with a thin wall, most commonly found in the head and neck area of an infant. Source: The Fetal Medicine Foundation, Education, Fetal Abnormalities, Neck, "Cystic Hygroma."
[3] Amniocentesis is a prenatal procedure where a small sample of amniotic fluid is extracted from the amniotic sac surrounding a developing fetus. Conducted between the fifteenth and twentieth weeks of pregnancy, the fluid is analyzed for genetic conditions. Source: The American College of Obstetricians and Gynecologists, FAQs, "Amniocentesis."

amniotic fluid is taken to check for genetic conditions. While Baby A appeared fine for now, a clear diagnosis would only come post-amniocentesis.

The subsequent two days were a blur of tears and debilitating anxiety, making even the simple act of getting out of bed an insurmountable task. The reality that even with favorable amnio results, there was still a 50% chance of birth defects weighed heavily. However, on a more optimistic note, a 15% chance remained that the cystic hygroma might dissipate on its own, and Baby B could emerge completely healthy.

I threw myself into researching the best fetal medicine specialists in Canada and the United States, finally locating one in Philadelphia close to Maureen and Jeff. Almost immediately, Kenny and I were engaged in a teleconference with a genetic counselor. We meticulously went through the risks and probabilities, and the counselor pointed out that experiencing complications with multiples in pregnancy is not uncommon. This was not just a theoretical risk assessment; it was our reality, unfolding in real time. I could no longer hang on to the safety net; I had to release my grip and face the uncertainty head-on, as terrifying as it was.

Days later, our plane touched down in Philadelphia, and I was a knotted mess of hope and despair. Somehow, I managed to avoid throwing up during the flight, a minor victory.

Dr. Eugene was a stoic figure, professional but empathetic. When Baby A appeared on the screen, my vision blurred with tears. The heartbreaking reality soon followed: Baby B had severe medical complications, and continuing with their development posed a critical threat to Baby A. The agonizing decision to reduce Baby B was made, an ordeal lasting only a few minutes but feeling like an eternity. Dr. Eugene reassured us that Baby B would be reabsorbed into the surrogate's uterus, and thankfully, Baby A remained unaffected. A Chorionic Villus Sampling (CVS)[4] test for Baby A was scheduled for later that week to ensure no chromosomal abnormalities were present. This was not simply an ultrasound; it was a diagnostic procedure akin to an amniocentesis. A sample of the placenta would be taken to test for genetic disorders. The goal now was to reach a point where the remaining pregnancy could progress smoothly.

The entire landscape had changed. No longer buoyed by unbridled excitement, our focus now turned sharply toward safeguarding the well-being of Baby A. The upcoming CVS test loomed as a gateway; should we pass through it unscathed, perhaps we could return to a semblance of the joyful anticipation that had marked the early days of this pregnancy—even if the imprint of loss would forever accompany us.

As I write this book, I cannot help but acknowledge the stark contrast between our experience and the current reproductive climate in the United States. If we faced the same circumstances today, would we have the same options? This was a real-life scenario where we needed to reduce Baby B to ensure the survival of Baby A. This decision came well beyond the six-week mark. How can a country that prides itself on principles of freedom and bravery strip away a woman's right to make decisions about her own body? Is this the portrait of

---

[4] Chorionic Villus Sampling (CVS) is a prenatal test where a small sample of cells, called chorionic villi, is taken from the placenta to test for specific genetic disorders in the fetus. Source: Johns Hopkins Medicine, Health: Treatments, Tests and Therapies, "Chorionic Villus Sampling (CVS)."

freedom? It's disheartening to observe such overt patriarchal interference cloaked in cowardice.

October 4, 2002

> We got the CVS results and—breathe out—everything is fine. We're expecting a healthy baby boy! I was so flooded with joy and relief that I couldn't help but add to the years-long reservoir of tears I'd already shed.
>
> We're approaching the fifteen-week mark on Monday, and the April due date still feels eons away. We've scheduled a trip to Harrisburg, Pennsylvania, to be with Maureen for the twenty-week ultrasound. She had just undergone her fourteen-week scan, and all signs pointed to a healthy progression.
>
> Though memories of Baby B continue to shadow my thoughts, I find reassurance in the conviction that we made the right choice. We're leaning toward the name Aidan Jakob for our son. "Aidan," with its Irish roots, means "little fire," encapsulating passion and vitality. "Jakob," in homage to Kenny's grandmother, my great-grandfather, and derived from Hebrew, signifies "supplanter," which reflects wisdom and growth. Together, the name Aidan Jakob represents a balanced blend of fiery energy and thoughtful evolution—how poignant.

November 23, 2002

> The rhythm of my journal entries has slowed, a sign perhaps of the peace that has settled over me. Each day, my thoughts drift numerous times to our baby growing in Maureen's womb.

We've crossed the halfway point, now at twenty-two weeks, and the reality sinks in with a mixture of awe and disbelief.

Back on November 2, Kenny and I had boarded a small propeller plane for a short flight to Harrisburg, PA, where we had the privilege of visiting our surrogate in the comfort of her own home. I'd planned to write while airborne, but the confined space and my spiraling nausea made that impossible. The mere sight of the cramped plane almost had me reconsidering the trip altogether. Any thought of putting pen to paper was snuffed out by my gut's revolt and my racing heart. Had the purpose of the trip not been so essential—to witness the development of our unborn son—I might have considered calling it off before the wheels even left the runway.

Upon arriving in Harrisburg, we first settled into a motel and soon after made our way to Maureen and Jeff's home. As she welcomed us inside, the comforting smell of a homemade dinner wafting from the oven enveloped us—a hearty aroma that instantly calmed my jittery nerves.

The moment that truly anchored me, however, was the sight of her rounded belly—our son's temporary home. As my eyes landed on the curve of her abdomen, I felt joy mingled with apprehension, eagerness intertwined with awe. For a second, everything else in the room seemed to fade into a blurry backdrop, leaving only this profound focal point.

As we sat down on the sofa, my hands felt inexplicably pulled toward her. It was as if they had their own yearning to connect with our son. I reached out and placed them gently but firmly on her abdomen. The tactile sensation of her warm skin under my fingertips, coupled with the slight movements beneath, was electric. It was as though I was trying to say, "I'm here, and I'm your mom," without uttering a single word. As my hands rested there, I hoped that each touch reverberated through her body and reached him. I wanted him to sense my presence, my love, and my fervent readiness for the life we would share. With every nerve in my body alight, it was as though I was already whispering love into his tiny, forming ears. As I felt him kick, I gently guided Kenny's hand to Maureen's stomach. A subtle yet powerful sensation, feeling like our son was communicating with us, letting us know in his own way that he felt our nearness and connection.

The appointment with Maureen's OB/GYN, Dr. Joyce, was scheduled in the same hospital where our son is to be born. The ultrasound revealed his growing form and heartbeat, which was a relief and an absolute joy to behold and hear. Dr. Joyce also showed us the remains of the other fetus, now being absorbed back into the uterus. While the sight was a sobering reminder of what we'd lost, the elation of seeing our healthy son eclipsed any remaining sorrow.

The journey into the twenty-fourth week—the sixth month—of pregnancy was a significant milestone. The ultrasound picture beamed back an image of vitality: our little warrior weighed a solid one pound, six ounces. Each new update deepened my connection to him, amplifying the anticipation of the moment he would be in my arms. Maureen described him as a bundle of energy, keeping her awake at night with his spirited movements and prompting numerous bathroom visits.

As January approached, my enthusiasm for setting up the nursery intensified. It became a cherished project that brought some brightness to the winter days. Tucked away in storage were treasures from Hannah's early days—a sturdy car seat, a snug baby chair, and a collection of soft, plush baby blankets. Reassembling her crib was a profoundly emotional experience. It felt as if we were coming full circle, with each piece we connected becoming a healing fragment of our story. Bit by bit, the nursery came together.

Around the same time, Maureen mentioned the intriguing possibility of us embarking on another pregnancy using our frozen embryos. The idea of planning another chapter while the current one was still unfolding was overwhelming, yet it expanded our sense of what could be possible for the future. If we decided to venture down that path again, Maureen would unquestionably be our first choice for a surrogate.

Dearest Reader: Can you recall a time in your life when immense joy overshadowed a loss, or perhaps a loss cast a shadow over a joyous occasion? How did you cope?

MILE 19

BETWEEN TWO WORLDS

When we began to share our joyful news with friends and family, the majority were elated while a handful were taken aback. They questioned our decision to maintain privacy for so long. One particular interaction stood out for its painful oversimplification. A casual acquaintance remarked offhandedly, "Wow, you're so lucky! You're having a baby and you're not going to gain any weight!" Her words momentarily robbed me of a response, reducing what we had been through to a shallow observation about physique. Walking away, I couldn't help but pity her limited perspective.

My emotions surrounding pregnancy and motherhood reclaimed center stage during a lunch with a pregnant friend. She was expecting her baby in June, and as I watched her hand instinctively rest on her expanding belly, a rush of feelings washed over me. Every time she described the gentle nudges and flutters she felt from within, I was consumed by envy, longing, and a touch of sadness. It's a tactile, intimate experience I can only vicariously sense. Yet even in that moment, a thought kept echoing softly in the back of my mind: *April isn't so far away, and soon I, too, will hold my baby close.*

December 12, 2002

HAPPY 33RD BIRTHDAY, KENNY!

I found it fitting to initiate this third journal with a passage shared with me over a year ago. It left a lasting impression. Written by an anonymous gestational surrogate, the words encapsulate a complexity and authenticity that deeply resonate with me, so similar to my own experience. Despite my best efforts to identify the original author, she remains unknown.

> "I will be having a baby in just a few days. This is not my baby. His expectant parents live about 200 miles from me. I am his surrogate mother, and I am coming to the end of my time with this miracle baby. Many people that I know very well and quite a few that I don't know well at all think that I am doing something wonderful and selfless by carrying someone else's child. Many people think that it is an awesome gift, a great sacrifice. I couldn't disagree more. There are many people involved in this relationship. It took a great many people, from counselors, to our agency, lawyers to medical experts, to make this vision of this child a reality. I want to shout from the rooftops who is the ultimate hero in this situation. I want the world to know who grieved, sacrificed and endured much more than occasional queasiness and some swelling. That person is the baby's mother.
>
> This baby's mother had to accept her inability to carry her own child inside of her. She made the decision that her love for a child that was not yet created could overcome her not having the baby grow in her own belly. She went to

professionals who needed to talk with her about the most intimate and private financial, medical and physiological matters. She researched and learned about things that she never realized were possible. She knew that she had a baby waiting for her.

When we spoke on the phone for the first time, we were complete strangers. There were certain things we needed to learn about each other that sometimes take close friends years to learn. She was aware that I knew much more about her than she did about me. She told me about the heartbreak of infertility that she knew I could never fully understand. When we met in person for the first time to talk further about intimate things that I'm sure some of her family knows nothing about, she was honest and vulnerable, and she cried.

As months went by, we planned for a pregnancy, and we grew closer. I can only imagine what it was like for her to learn to trust me. She knew that, hopefully, I would be helping them to have the baby that she longed for. I knew at times that she was worried about me liking her. She never needed to worry.

We made decisions together that are never made in any other situation. She was by my side when the doctor put her baby inside me, and I know with all my heart that she wanted it to be her, but she had a goal in her heart. She had a baby waiting for her.

She had to rely on me to tell her about any symptoms that I may be having as we waited to find out if we were pregnant or not. She had to know that I would be the first one to know if she would have a baby. She had to learn from me if she was expecting or if she needed to brace herself for heartbreaking disappointment.

We did find out that she was expecting a child, but she had to experience all of the symptoms of pregnancy through me. Her baby was far away from her with me and my family. She had to trust that I was taking my medications as needed. She had to know that I was being careful with my body that held a part of her. She needed to rely on me to let her know what the medical professionals were telling me about our pregnancy. We learned that she was expecting twins, only to later learn that we had lost one of the babies she already loved. She had to share her grief with me. Nothing would be only hers and hers alone with this pregnancy.

As her baby and my belly grew, her mixture of happiness, excitement, fear and envy must have been unbearable at times. As she shared the news of her baby with family, friends and neighbors, she had to report events and feelings second-hand, similar to an expectant father but much more difficult. She could not see me every day, sleep with the baby and feel my growing belly every night. She had to try to be lucky enough to catch her baby moving so she could feel him when we were together.

The wonders, both physical and physiological, that I have experienced with this pregnancy are ones that I will cherish forever. There is no feeling in this world like a life growing inside you. To feel the baby moving, see him at our doctor's appointments, and share with strangers my due date and how I'm feeling. I love all of this, but it is mixed with sadness. The sadness comes with the knowledge that this baby's mother had to give these things to me. Letting me experience it makes me sad because I know that she feels what she is missing. She has endured her baby growing in her heart instead of her uterus. She has braved the questions when shopping in the baby section about her due date and why her stomach is so beautifully flat.

I know our relationship is about to change. I have some fears myself. I cannot express how much I have enjoyed sharing my life with this baby's mother. I know that soon she will not need me as she has the past year, and I have already started to selfishly miss her dependency on me. I now realize that I've become dependent on her. Our goal of the past year is about to be realized, and I get to see my vision of having her take over caring for her baby and taking him home come true. She will get to look into her baby's eyes and exhale. I will witness her holding her baby in her arms and inhaling his scent. I also know, with a bit of grief but mostly pride, that she will not need me anymore. I couldn't be happier for her.

I am the fortunate one. I am the one who has gotten to know someone so courageous and so beautiful. I have witnessed incredible feats of love and courage from someone who I don't think even realizes what an amazing mother she has already been to this baby. I get to cherish the rest of my life that the baby I had a small part of will be with someone who moved Heaven and Earth and sacrificed so much to bring him into the world. I know he will grow to know how lucky he is. I also know with all of my heart how lucky I am to have been a part of this growing family.

I will never be able to thank her enough for what she has brought to me and my family. I will forever be grateful to her for sharing her life with me and honoring me by carrying a part of her heart for these past nine months. She has shown me motherhood as I would have never seen it by raising my own miracles. She has been an awesome example of selflessness, courage, grace and love. She is my hero." —Anonymous

February 25, 2003

Returning from Harrisburg, PA, the experience still lingers with me: the tactile sensation of touching Maureen's belly, the scent of sanitized hospital halls, and the evocative imagery on the 4D ultrasound screen. Aidan is steadily growing at 4.5 pounds. Seeing his face with such clarity was nothing short of a visual embrace; it was as if he was already part of our immediate world.

As my hands rested on Maureen's abdomen, I silently willed Aidan to sense my presence. To somehow feel the intense, endless love that radiated from the palms of my hands into his tiny, growing body. In this unique journey, I often felt caught between two worlds. One world where my heart felt every beat, every flutter, and the other where the physical distance magnified every moment of separation. I was a mother, connected deeply to my child, yet separated by the circumstances of our path. It was an interplay between joy and longing, presence and absence.

During the hospital tour, our footsteps echoed on the polished linoleum floors as we inspected the birthing rooms. The atmosphere was a juxtaposition of antiseptic sterility and anticipatory warmth. A kind head nurse guided us. Given our unique arrangement with Maureen as our surrogate, it was imperative to solidify our roles. I felt a sense of urgency to make it clear that Kenny and I would be making all the health-related decisions for Aidan while he was in the hospital's care.

Maureen's OB gave us a gentle outline: induction is planned for the thirty-ninth week. It was a straightforward statement, yet one that sent emotional ripples through me. This isn't just a day on a calendar; it's a portal to our future.

I sit here, in the room we've prepared for Aidan, swaying on the glider and debating the finer points of crib bedding. Even as we progress further into this pregnancy—beyond the point when Hannah was born—the shadow of fear continues to haunt me. The mere thought of encountering any snags or complications feels unbearable to even contemplate.

Hannah can't wait to be a big sister, and Kenny, ever the stalwart, reassures me. Yet, the waiting feels eternal. Aidan, every day, every moment, I send my love your way, hoping you'll feel it, hoping you'll already know me when we finally meet. I feel a connection so intrinsic, it's as if I can sense your every move, as if you were a part of me.

Today, the official Birth Order[1] arrived. By the law of the State of Pennsylvania, you are unequivocally ours: Alison Beder Solway, your mother; Kenneth M. Solway, your father.

Dearest Reader: Have you ever faced a situation where you had to accept something beyond your control? How did you transform it into a strength?

---

[1] A Prebirth Parentage Order is a court-issued legal document that establishes the intended parents as the legal parents of a child prior to birth, commonly used in surrogacy arrangements. This order aims to clarify parental rights, thus preventing potential legal disputes post-birth. Source: reproductivelawyer.com, "Birth Orders."

MILE 20

A REBIRTH

March 5, 2003. Seated alone on a plane headed for Philadelphia, within me echoed the adage adapted from Robert Burns: "Even the best-laid plans often go awry." Kenny stayed in Toronto to be with Hannah and was set to fly into Harrisburg on March 7. My emotions were a tempest, heavily dominated by apprehension but threaded with stubborn hope. Laryngitis had reduced my voice to a raspy whisper, and a looming headache made its presence known. As the plane idled on the runway due to a snowstorm, I felt caught in limbo. I sent silent prayers for clear skies over Philadelphia while getting some relief from the Dramamine I'd taken. When we finally ascended, the snowstorm was left behind, but my internal tumult remained.

A mere week before, Maureen had been hospitalized, presenting a medley of disconcerting symptoms: a swollen leg, a pervasive feeling of malaise, and tests revealing elevated protein levels coupled with heightened blood pressure. Although she was discharged with instructions for strict bed rest, the incident deepened the shadows of my anxieties.

The day after I arrived, I joined Maureen at the hospital, where her OB had lined up crucial tests—an ultrasound and an amniocentesis—to assess whether the baby was ready for birth. The results were expected the next day. Filled with

A Rebirth

cautious optimism, we hoped for positive outcomes. Should all indicators point in the right direction, particularly Aidan's lung maturity, the doctor planned to induce labor on March 8—a date that held personal significance for me, as it would have marked the birthday of my late grandfather, Papa Monte.

On Friday, March 7, at 8:10 a.m., my phone, always within arm's reach, rang with the anticipated call from Maureen. "We're a go!" My heart danced, torn between the thrill of the news and its associated apprehensions.

After picking up Kenny from the Harrisburg airport that same morning, we made our way to the hospital and arrived by 11 a.m. A gel was applied to Maureen's cervix to prepare her for the following day, and her contractions, although slight, began with startling immediacy.

The medical team surpassed all expectations by including us in every detail, with the exception of Maureen's primary obstetrician, Dr. Joyce. Despite his undeniable competence, his manner often made me feel more like an afterthought than an essential participant. His confidence, tipping at times into condescension, relegated me to the sidelines. Yet, I chose to remain silent, prioritizing my son's well-being above all. Accepting Dr. Joyce's demeanor, however grating it might have been, seemed a small price to pay for ensuring a safe delivery.

Given the immediate reaction to the gel and the concerning distance between Maureen's house and the hospital, we decided that Maureen and Jeff should stay at our hotel, across the street. That evening, we ventured to a steakhouse—which, in hindsight, may not have been the best pre-delivery meal decision.

It was March 8, the day we had long awaited: 1,436 days, to be exact. Today we would welcome our baby boy. We arrived at Harrisburg Hospital at 8:30 a.m. Our surrogate's Pitocin drip, meant to induce labor, was administered by an exceptionally compassionate nurse. Dr. Joyce came in later to assess Maureen's cervix, measuring it at one to two centimeters. He said if there was no progress, he would return in a few hours to break her water. Given that her contractions weren't particularly strong, I didn't expect things to move quickly in the next few hours. Kenny, visibly fatigued, found a chair and succumbed to some much-needed sleep.

In the hush of the previous night, my quest for sleep had been continually thwarted. An unexpected coughing fit jolted me awake at 1:20 a.m., shattering the quiet of the room. However, that disturbance was about to be overshadowed. At 2:00 a.m., against the muffled acoustics of the bathroom door, Kenny's voice, laced with discomfort, came through. He spoke of a persistent ache in his chest. While he was worried it might be a heart attack (despite no other symptoms), I recognized it as acid reflux. I knew Kenny all too well, and thanks to those paper-thin walls, I also couldn't mistake the symphony of unfortunate sounds—it was clear he was hosting a diarrhea disco in there, a classic case of digestive distress. *Do I laugh or cry?* "Remember the blooming onion and that mammoth steak you ate for dinner?" I said, my voice dripping with faux innocence. "Sounds like they're staging an uprising."

Seeing his turmoil, I proposed, "If you're truly worried, walk over to the ER. It's right across the street." Trying to tread the line between jest and genuine care, I added, "While you might think it's a heart attack, I'm betting on

Montezuma's revenge." From our hotel window, I watched him make the short trek to the ER, each step heavy with both concern and the weight of that ill-fated dinner.

Sleep remained elusive for me the rest of the night. After a lengthy five-hour assessment, Kenny's grand diagnosis was... indigestion, just as I had suspected. As dawn broke, he reappeared, slightly humbled yet relieved, clutching a Maalox bottle like a soldier returning with a medal from battle.

At 3:20 p.m., Kenny was revitalized and alert as Maureen's water broke. The atmosphere was charged with expectancy and thrill—we were on the verge of welcoming our baby boy into the world.

Maureen's labor progressed with a slow but steady grace, her calm demeanor defying the physical toll it took on her body. The epidural dulled the sharpness of each contraction, allowing her to focus on the work at hand. Instead of a room filled with struggle, it was an atmosphere of anticipation and quiet strength, setting the stage for Aidan's entrance into the world. Jeff was at Maureen's side with Kenny and me, the three of us each in our own way lending our strength to her.

Dr. Joyce moved with practiced expertise, giving Maureen his full attention—which was undoubtedly crucial. Yet, his total disregard for my presence reduced me to the role of an unnoticed observer, despite being the soon-to-be mother. In that moment, I reminded myself of my focus, my one paramount desire: the healthy arrival of Aidan.

Kenny stood behind me, his hands resting gently but firmly on my shoulders, as if anchoring me to the floor. And I needed it. My legs wavered, a quiver stemming not from the sterile brightness of hospital lights or the surgical steel tools laid out like a medieval armory, but from the sheer surealness of the moment. Witnessing the birth of our flesh and blood was an out-of-body experience; it felt like floating above an extraordinary event that dwarfed everything I'd ever known.

When Aidan's head crowned—his hair spangled with the fluids of birth—I felt tears surging behind my eyelids. One escaped, trickling down my cheek. I blinked it away, steadying myself. This was not the time for collapse. I had to be a pillar, for both our surrogate and the tiny life about to join us.

I remember the sensory burst when Aidan finally emerged: the sharp snip of the umbilical cord, the sanitized air of the room replaced by the new, raw scent of life, and the immediate absence of tension, like the aftermath of a storm. Nurses whisked Aidan away with seamless efficiency, honoring him with the inaugural rituals of his earthly existence: cleaning, measuring, and marveling. Born at 8:57 p.m., he was a modest yet perfect 6.9 pounds and measured 19 inches in length, but the statistics couldn't capture the enormity of his presence.

As Kenny and I stood beside Aidan's bassinet, a tremor of uncertainty undermined my elation. There he was—our son, a tapestry of years woven into one miraculous being. And yet, the anxieties that had long stalked me felt as though they were hovering, fragile spectres awaiting one last chance to haunt me. I pinched the flesh of my arm, half anticipating the cruel awakening from what I so fervently wished was not an ephemeral dream. It was then that the nurse locked eyes with me, her gaze a lighthouse piercing through my fog of disbelief. "Sweetheart, it's okay," she said, her voice imbued with a kindness that felt almost maternal. "He is indeed real, and he's yours."

Her words were like a spell, banishing the last remnants of my fear, affirming that this, all of this, was as true as the tears that blurred my vision. Aidan was not just an abstract wish or a figment of desperate yearning. He was our reality—impossibly beautiful and entirely, irrevocably ours.

I cried, unrestrained, as I softly touched Aidan's minute fingers. Each contour of his skin felt like a love letter written in Braille. Behind me, Kenny's steadfast grip was my ballast, reassuring me that I wouldn't dissolve under the enormity of my feelings.

As the nurse placed Aidan into my arms, a wave of relief, joy, and amazement swept over me. I caught Maureen's eye and whispered, "Thank you," realizing that those two words could never fully capture the depth of my gratitude. The love I felt was something I hadn't experienced since Hannah's birth.

Cradling Aidan, I called my parents, my voice trembling, hamstrung by the swell of sentiments that defied articulation. Their joy echoed ours, amplifying the preciousness of this irreplaceable moment. Kenny, too, shared the news with his family, his tone carrying both fatigue and elation. We had crossed the threshold, becoming parents once more to a radiant baby boy.

The hospital staff in both the Labor and Delivery and the Maternity Wards were simply wonderful, embodying competence and compassion. As Aidan was guided into the nursery, Kenny and I watched in awe. The nurses carefully gave him his first sponge bath, and we marveled at how something so simple could feel so monumental. Meanwhile,

Maureen and Jeff were doing well as she settled into her recovery room.

Aidan was to remain under observation for the next few hours. Although I didn't want to leave him alone, the nurses encouraged us to catch up on some much-needed rest at the hotel. When we returned to the hospital at 7 a.m., we were shown to a room on the maternity floor. It was in that humble space that Aidan, Kenny, and I began to understand each other, filling the room with a curious mix of serenity and constant discovery that only new parents and infant could truly understand.

That morning of March 9, 2003, our pediatrician gave us the go-ahead to bring Aidan home. Maureen was also being discharged, and as we prepared to part ways, complex feelings welled up inside me. Our eyes met, and it felt as though words would be too clumsy to convey the gratitude and love that filled the room. "I don't even know how to begin thanking you," I stammered.

Maureen smiled, her own eyes shining with emotion. "Alison, carrying Aidan was an honor. He's so fortunate to have you and Kenny as parents."

We hugged tightly, each aware that this was a farewell but not a goodbye, the promise of an enduring friendship between us. "We'll speak soon," I said.

The drive to Philadelphia kicked off with Aidan comfortably ensconced in his car seat. At the airport, I moved with meticulous care, finding a secluded corner for his feeding. I cradled Aidan in my arms, draping a baby blanket over him to shield from the surrounding bustle and potential germs. Oblivious to my heightened state, he slept peacefully throughout the flight, his calm presence dispelling my fears about his comfort and ear pressure.

Our passage through immigration was unexpectedly smooth. The Canadian officials, as if sensing the weight of our poignant journey, processed our papers with an evident gentleness. When I reached the baggage claim, I felt as though I'd crossed an emotional finish line. A whirl of relief, happiness, and the settling realization that we were now, in every way that counted, home.

As we emerged through the sliding glass doors of the airport, my father was there, waiting to pick us up. His smile was immense, a genuine expression of pure joy, his eyes full of tears. It was a privilege to witness him meeting his grandson for the first time. Thinking back on that experience still moves me deeply.

Walking in the front door with Aidan, we were greeted by blue and white balloons floating like bubbles of happiness. Welcome Home signs, crafted by Hannah with heartfelt care, covered the walls, transforming our house into a celebratory embrace. Her excitement was palpable, her feet barely touching the floor as she bounced up and down.

"He's so tiny," she exclaimed, her eyes widening with awe.

"Would you like to hold him?" I gently lifted Aidan from his car seat and swaddled him in a soft blanket before carefully handing him to Hannah, who was already seated on the couch, her eager arms extended in readiness. As Aidan settled into her lap, their eyes met in a silent, momentous exchange. A sense of profound peace washed over me, as if I could glimpse their future—a lifetime filled with laughter, shared secrets, and unwavering support. It left me convinced that they would have a sibling bond as strong and as enriching as the one I treasure with Adam and Aarin.

Sharing the moment with my parents and in-laws made it even more special; their faces were glowing with joy as they welcomed their newest grandson. Adam and his then-fiancée, Lindsey, joined us, adding to the family warmth, and Aarin called from university, her voice choked with emotion over not being there in person, yet thrilled all the same. And standing amid it all, I felt a renewed sense of wonder at the beautiful complexity of life.

May 23, 2003

Eleven weeks. It's hard to believe Aidan has been with us for that long. It's surreal—feeling as if he's always been stitched into the matrix of our universe. He's probably crossed the twelve-pound mark—our little wonder is growing by the day. When he smiles, the world seems to burst into color. I find it challenging to encapsulate the warmth that radiates from my heart, filling every inch of my being.

His coos are his own unique language—tiny vocal fireworks that make every day a celebration. Those soulful big eyes and petal-soft lips have me captivated. His locks of light brown hair seem to carry the last glow of sunset.

Hannah has transitioned into a big sister like she was born for it. "Look, Mommy, Aidan's smiling!" she says, her voice full of admiration and affection. She's more than just a marvel; she's a young girl with an uncanny, almost maternal, knack for sibling care. It's remarkable, really, how seamlessly she's

A Rebirth

integrated Aidan into her life. Observing her, I see reflections of myself, recalling how I was with Aarin.

A year ago, in this very room, I sent up prayers like invisible threads woven with hope. Fast-forward to today, and I see Aidan, comfortably asleep as if he's always known this world, resting snugly on Kenny's shoulder.

The Bris[1] ceremony for Aidan was an emotional bookmark. His brief discomfort tested my resolve. Amid the gathering of loved ones, Kenny and I voiced our hopes, our words thick with sentiment: "May you navigate life with curiosity and courage." Hannah, with a mature depth in her young voice, declared, "You're already my favorite person."

Maureen, our wonderful surrogate, is doing well. She recently sent us a heartfelt note along with a beautiful baby blanket—a gesture that felt like a meaningful keepsake from a life-altering journey we shared. She also delicately broached the subject of another surrogacy, a notion that has quietly resonated with me.

We have four frozen embryos at AFS, each brimming with untapped potential. As I look at Aidan and Hannah, I can't help but wonder, Could another life join this intricate dance of ours? It's a quiet what-if, lingering neither urgently nor dismissively.

---

[1] A Bris is a Jewish religious ceremony that involves the circumcision of a baby boy on the eighth day after his birth. The ritual is a covenant between the Jewish people and God and is considered a significant rite of passage within the Jewish community. Source: *Encyclopedia Judaica*, "Circumcision."

As for the ache of not carrying my own children, it's becoming a distant island, fading slowly into the horizon of my past. Right here, right now, life feels gloriously full. Yet, a whisper inside suggests our family's narrative might have more chapters to write and more love to both give and receive.

"Dearest Alison & Kenny,

Hi, guys! I hope this card finds you well and settling into your new life with baby Aidan.

I can hardly believe we've reached the end of this extraordinary journey. Over the course of eleven long months, it has been my privilege to get to know you both, as well as your delightful daughter, Hannah. It's hard to put into words how much this experience has meant to me.

Thank you for entrusting me with the most precious cargo imaginable. You both showed me nothing but love and kindness throughout this process, and I never felt judged or secondary.

Alison, your emotional support during the challenging times of this pregnancy has been invaluable. I can't express enough how grateful I am for your compassion and empathy. You've done so much more for me than you had to, and never once made me feel like you were only concerned about Aidan.

Saying goodbye was tough, but knowing the immense love that awaits Aidan in his new home made it a bit easier. He has the most wonderful parents a little boy could ask for. I've enjoyed him for the last 9 months; now it's your turn to enjoy him for a lifetime.

If you ever decide that your family is still incomplete, you know where to find me! It would be my honor to accompany you on this incredible journey once again.

You, Kenny, Hannah, and Aidan will forever hold a special place in my heart and life.

Love Always, M. xox"

Crossing the finish line of a race brings an unmistakable euphoria. You're engulfed in pride, accomplishment, and relief. In that moment, the idea of a next race doesn't cross your mind. For me, it's a time to savor the completion, basking in the thought of not having to endure such a challenge again. But, as time moves on and recovery sets in, your focus gradually shifts. You start pondering future goals, contemplating races that could be more challenging, easier, or similar to the last. The breathlessness at the finish line fades into memory, replaced by the lingering sense of triumph. That's when the search for the next starting line begins, readying yourself for another test of endurance and achievement.

Dearest Reader: What if, for a moment, you close your eyes and visualize the perfect ending to your own chapter? How does that feel? What have you gained?

PART IV

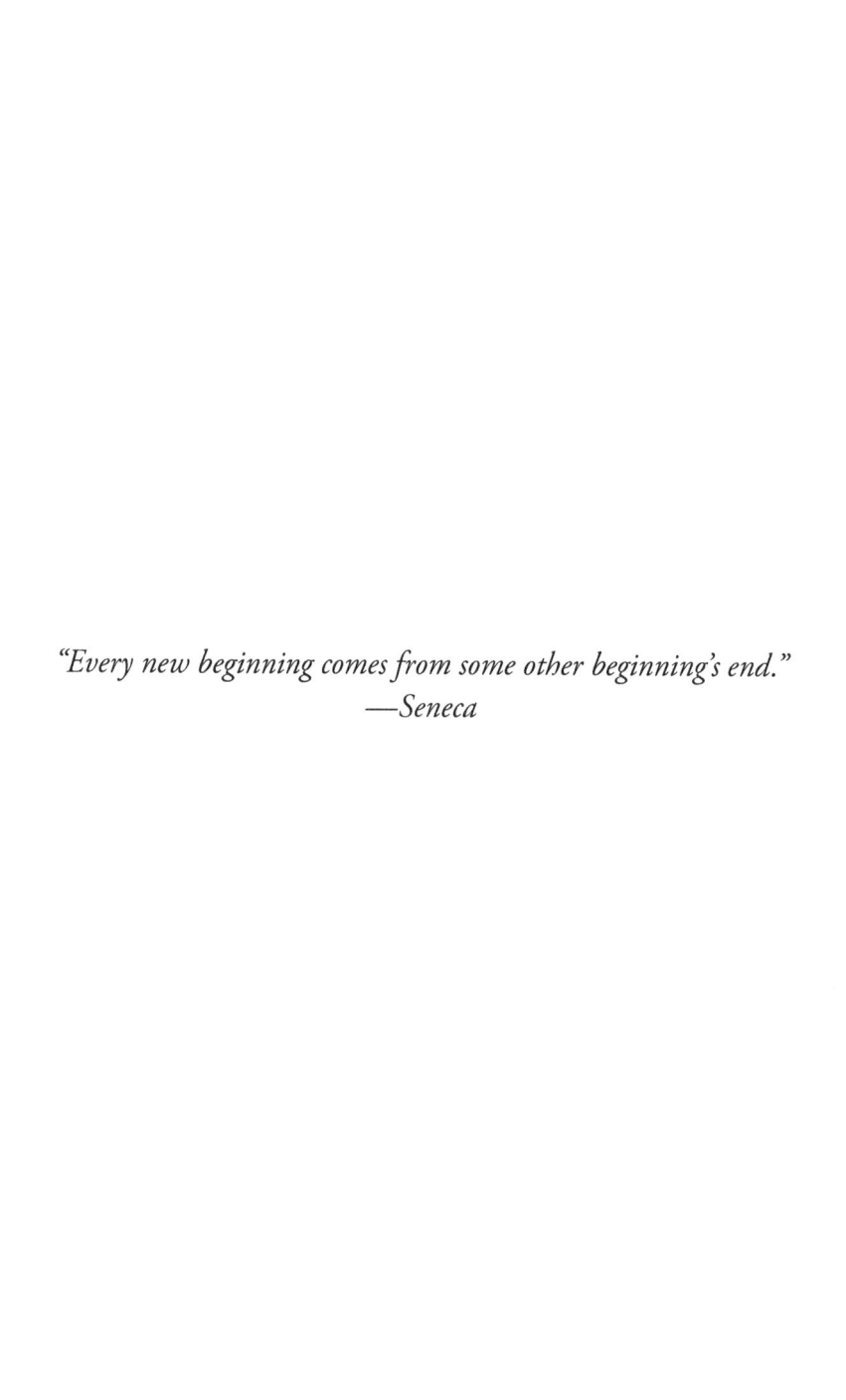

"Every new beginning comes from some other beginning's end."
—*Seneca*

MILE 21

HERE WE GO AGAIN

It had been almost a year. Each morning as I entered Aidan's room, the radiance of his wide eyes and the curve of his smile dissolved me into a state of pure elation. Every *Mommy*, each *Daddy*, all the laughter, and the milestones achieved—these were moments of unfiltered joy. Witnessing the synergy between Aidan and Hannah was like discovering two puzzle pieces that completed a long-unfinished picture. This filled me with an inexplicable sense of calm but also left me pondering: *Is our family truly complete, or is there room for another addition?*

This thought had crystallized one morning as I stepped out of the shower. On the bathroom wall, a peculiar shadow caught my eye—a shape that resembled a womb, with two smaller forms that looked like fetuses enclosed within it—suspended in time. Struck by the unexpected vision, I whispered, "Is this a sign?"

Kenny and I settled into a serious conversation, weighing our options like a scale seeking balance. At AFS, four frozen embryos held the potential for a third child, a possibility I couldn't easily dismiss. I understood, though, that if these embryos proved unviable after thawing or failed to result in a pregnancy, we wouldn't embark on another fresh cycle.

As we deliberated, I couldn't help but acknowledge the immense richness that Hannah and Aidan had already brought into our lives. Hannah had literally saved my life, forcing an end to a pregnancy that my heart could no longer sustain. Aidan, too, had his own form of rescue—his presence reignited a courage within me and served as a living testament to the resilience of hope. I recognized that if fate decided that our family was to remain as four, I would embrace that reality.

We were fully cognizant of the financial ramifications of expanding our household. Yet, the unwavering support from our families made another surrogacy endeavor possible—a privilege we didn't take lightly. Without their backing, the monetary burden would have been insurmountable.

Articulating the compelling draw I felt toward those remaining embryos isn't straightforward. As I started to regain trust in my intuition—a sense that I feared I'd lost—I felt increasingly certain. My gut told me that our family was not yet complete.

We first talked about the possibility with Maureen during a pivotal conversation in February. She was equally eager. Although our initial thought was to start in the fall, Maureen preferred early spring. Not wanting to lose her to another couple due to a seasonal timing issue, we readily agreed.

As the weeks unfolded between that February discussion and our targeted April transfer, we immersed ourselves in meticulous planning. Medical histories were updated, key consultations arranged, and imminent obstacles carefully weighed. This groundwork had us approaching spring with a heightened sense of readiness—a feeling amplified by another remarkable milestone: Aidan's first birthday.

The early March celebration filled our home with the laughter and warmth of family and friends. Aidan was a walking, talking embodiment of friendliness. When he took his first bite of birthday cake—cake that ended up as much on his face as in his mouth—his eyes widened in sugary astonishment.

Meanwhile, Hannah became his petite guardian, exemplifying her infinite affection. Whether she was wrestling with his diaper tabs, gently spooning pureed vegetables into his mouth, or giving him underdog pushes on the park swing, her attentiveness to him never faltered. Seeing them share not just activities but emotions—joy, frustration, curiosity—wove a fabric of togetherness that expanded the boundaries of my heart.

What had previously been purely theoretical began to take concrete form. Maureen initiated her drug protocol, and I engaged in detailed discussions with Gillian, our dependable nurse at AFS, to finalize the timeline. If all went according to plan, the embryo transfer was set for the last week in April.

Impressively, everything felt more streamlined than our prior experience. I was noticeably calmer, devoid of the intense desperation that had previously consumed me. Yet, my aspirations this time around were as significant as they had been with Aidan. Deep down, I fervently wished for another healthy baby.

I was keenly aware of the significance of our four precious embryos preserved in frozen suspension. Having made the difficult decision not to undergo any further rounds of fertility medication or IVF cycles, I knew those embryos represented our remaining chances. Our current strategy centered on transferring two viable embryos, always with the understanding that the doctor's expertise might guide our final steps. In this critical juncture, with those four potential futures in the balance, we stood on the threshold of a new chapter, overflowing once again with hope and trepidation.

Embryo transfer days were like "race day." The early mornings, the long runs, the proper diet—they all form crucial parts of preparation, but on race day, when you're at the starting line, a different reality sets in. It's not just about the physical endurance anymore; it's about mental resilience, the ability to adapt to the unexpected, to find strength even when your body wants to give in. Similarly, our journey to parenthood, though diligently planned and greatly anticipated, brought with it unforeseen challenges and deep emotional complexities that we only truly understood as we experienced them firsthand.

April 25, 2004

As the engines roar to life and the plane ascends toward New Jersey, my chest swells. This flight isn't just a physical transition but an emotional pilgrimage. I close my eyes briefly, feeling as though we are breaking free from Earth's gravity in more ways than one. My fingers tighten around the armrest, knuckles whitening. A cold shiver runs down my spine, as if my vulnerabilities were momentarily exposed to the cabin's chill. This attempt is our final opportunity to welcome another life into our world.

My biological limitations loom large, casting long, indelible shadows over this process. I can't shake the unsettling notion that despite all the medical advances, all the careful planning, and even with Maureen's invaluable help, some things remain beyond my grasp. I can almost taste the bitterness of that truth—acrid yet grounding.

Should we falter, should these embryos not take hold in the nurturing environment that Maureen provides, my soul faces a heavy task: finding a new equilibrium, a place of peace and acceptance with my beautiful family of four. The gravity of that potential reality presses against my chest, making each breath feel heavier than the last. It's a weight I hope to never know, but one I must prepare to shoulder.

Putting these thoughts down in my journal, I breathe a little easier. Transferring the words from mind to paper seems to lessen their intensity and lighten their mental load. The act of journaling offers me a delicate yet invaluable solace—a space where fears and hopes coexist, neither one overpowering the other.

Meeting Maureen and Jeff in the hotel lobby felt like reconnecting with an old melody: the tune was familiar, but the rhythm had gained depth. Two years had passed since our initial meeting in Morristown, and it was as if time had fermented our shared experiences into something more potent—a blend of wisdom and insight. "You ready for tomorrow?" Maureen asked, her voice filled with eagerness, her eyes both seeking and offering reassurance. "Yes, we're more than ready," Kenny replied, his voice calm and determined.

The next morning, Kenny and I accompanied Jeff and Maureen to the clinic for her scan and blood work. When the news came that her lining was exactly where it needed to *be, we felt a wave of relief. Donning our scrubs, we waited for the doctor who would perform the transfer. Three out of the four embryos had survived the thaw.*

Unanimously, we agreed to transfer the remaining three. As I watched via ultrasound those tiny embryos travel into Maureen's uterus, gratitude, fear, and an overwhelming sense of finality surged through me. Our surrogate, in an act of boundless generosity, once again carried the very essence of my dreams.

The doctor offered encouraging odds, estimating a 60% to 70% chance of achieving a singleton pregnancy, which means one baby rather than multiples. I prayed with every fiber of my being that any of those three beautiful embryos would develop into a healthy baby. Meanwhile, my thoughts frequently drifted to Hannah and Aidan. I missed them immensely and couldn't wait to see their faces when we returned home the next day. And so, we had entered the infamous wait—a stretch of time defined by cautious optimism and restrained anticipation.

The ten-day waiting period had been an emotional seesaw, a crucible moment: either our family would grow, or it would remain a beautiful quartet. I was open to either possibility, but if I was being honest, a deep-seated longing for another child remained.

As the time for Maureen's call drew near, the clock seemed to slow down like it always did, each second stretching out as if reluctant to pass. My palms were damp; my heart was a rapid staccato in my chest. It was almost 1:30 p.m., and my fingers hovered over my phone. Kenny stood beside me, his presence a quiet fortress.

Then it came—Maureen's voice slicing through the knot of emotions: "We're pregnant!"

The words hit me like a bolt of pure joy. Tears escaped, flowing down my cheeks in an unstoppable torrent. Kenny wrapped me in his arms and in a single swift motion lifted me off the ground.

"We're having another baby!" he shouted, his voice tinged with a wonder that mirrored my own.

The next day's blood test, an hCG level of 241, hinted at twins. As the weeks unfolded, the numbers climbed—384, then over 800—fueling our eagerness for the upcoming doctor's appointment. Maureen's five-week ultrasound confirmed it: two sacs, two fetuses, and a cascade of emotions. All we could think of were the two tiny heartbeats we'd soon hear.

Twins weren't unfamiliar territory for us; we'd endured the difficulties of Aidan's pregnancy and had also faced the heartbreaking loss of identical twins with Amy. But this journey felt different—more familiar. It was as if fate had granted us a third act, a chance to dance to an old song but with fresh steps.

Almost skeptically, I questioned my abundance of luck. At the core, my family remained my anchor. Facing the idea of four children, I clung to the resilience that had carried us through past adversities. Almost four years after learning I couldn't carry any more children, here we were—still writing a story that defied all odds.

In the weighty air of a July morning, we found ourselves in the all-too-familiar environment of a hospital waiting room, albeit this time at St. Luke's Roosevelt Hospital in New York City. Dr. Eugene, our trusted medical adviser during Maureen's surrogacy with Aidan, had relocated to New York, prompting us to follow him there.

Given the complexities of our pregnancy with Aidan, we opted for a Chorionic Villus Sampling (CVS)—a prenatal test to detect birth defects—on both fetuses. Maureen offered a comforting smile, brimming with serene strength. Dr. Eugene, with his wealth of experience and familiarity, adeptly performed the procedure. The room was awash in a tense quietude, which Dr. Eugene finally dispelled when he spoke. "All seems in order," he affirmed. "We should have the initial results by tomorrow." This news prompted a collective sigh of relief, a moment of comfort amid an atmosphere still dense with apprehension and uncertainty.

The next day, we were at LaGuardia Airport, waiting for our flight back to Toronto, when my phone buzzed with the call we'd been anticipating. "Both CVS results were clear," the voice on the other end said. "And you're having two boys!" I looked at Kenny. We burst into a genuine, hearty laugh—filled with the overwhelming realization of our rapidly approaching future. A picture of our lives—overflowing with three boys under the age of two and four kids under six—flashed before my eyes. It promised a beautiful chaos, and we couldn't have been more thrilled.

As summer gave way to fall, the impending arrival of our twins became more real with each passing day. Maureen was feeling their movements—a phenomenon she described as "playful pokes" —and it filled my heart with an indescribable warmth.

When we arrived in Harrisburg for the twenty-week ultrasound, seeing Maureen was once again like a breath of fresh air. Her abdomen had visibly grown—each contour a reflection of the burgeoning life within. As with Aidan, I felt an irresistible urge to place my hands on her belly, where I sensed the subtle movements of our sons. Leaning in, I spoke softly to them: "We love you so much."

During the ultrasound, Kenny and I found ourselves holding our breath until the first blurry images materialized on the screen, showing two little beings, looking robust and full of promise. Once again, relief tinged with elation surged through me. The measurements clicked into place: normal, healthy, and promising. Baby A was the picture of tranquillity, while Baby B was a flurry of motion—a glimpse into their distinct personalities.

As I stood on the precipice of motherhood once more, I was met by some old friends: doubt and fear. Yet, deep within, there was a love so fierce and raw that had been born with Hannah and Aidan. This hope, resilient and powerful, pushed back against the shadows, assuring me that beyond the uncertainties, my immeasurable love awaited my boys.

Dearest Reader: Visualize the interplay between hope and skepticism in your life, especially when confronted with significant decisions or transformative experiences. What methods do you use to maintain this delicate balance?

MILE 22

TWO FOR THE ROAD

When I chose to run a marathon, my decision didn't fully sink in until I began telling others. Speaking it into existence felt like a contract; I was now irreversibly committed. The experience paralleled our announcement to extended family and friends about expecting twins. Once the words left our lips, the reality set in. There was no turning back; our lives were about to change in the most extraordinary way.

I had never envisioned a day when a minivan would spark joy in my heart, yet there we stood in the dealership, eyes glued to a gleaming new symbol of suburban surrender.

"This must be the chariot for those who've not only left coolness behind but sent it a 'wish you were here' postcard," I remarked.

Kenny laughed. "Welcome to the minivan club—first rule: forget you were ever cool."

As we signed the papers, all I could see ahead was a future filled with accumulated stray sippy cups, lost toys, and enough crumbs to sustain a small zoo.

I realized we would need duplicates of everything—two cribs, car seats, and a double stroller. Aidan was to move into what had been my office so the twins could occupy his more spacious room. As the January due date loomed closer, logistical preparations kicked into high gear. I had spoken with the head nurse at Harrisburg Hospital to ensure a seamless experience. Our lawyer was busy with the legal intricacies of the Birth Orders. Each task I checked off my list fueled my sense of purpose, transforming my anxious anticipation into a deep sense of fulfillment and tempered elation.

Hannah's initial disappointment about not gaining a sister had swiftly turned into delight at her newfound status as the sole girl—"You don't count, Mommy"—in a house full of boys. The energy in our home was electric as we all eagerly crossed off the days until our family would grow by four more feet. Reactions from friends mostly leaned toward encouragement, albeit with a sense of awe at the impending mayhem. But I was ready. I yearned for the joyous pandemonium that awaited me, eager to hold my sons and feel their boundless love.

For Baby A, we had settled on the name Caleb Monte. "Caleb," of Hebrew origin, signified devotion and wholeheartedness. "Monte," an Italian name meaning "mountain," honored my paternal grandfather—a meaningful connection heightened by the fact that Aidan also shares a birthday with him. For Baby B, we had decided on the name Rowen Alexander. "Rowen," derived from Celtic roots, symbolized vitality and a close bond with nature. "Alexander," a name of Greek origin meaning "defender of the people," was a tribute not only to my great-uncle Alex but also to Kenny's paternal grandfather.

We had entered our twenty-sixth week, and a thrill bubbled inside me each time I considered the twins' latest ultrasound—their approximate weight was two pounds each.

It was becoming so real. I couldn't wait to meet my beautiful boys.

November 30, 2004

Today marks the thirty-four-week milestone of our twin boys' impending arrival. The excitement is as clear as the crisp late-autumn air. Maureen is enduring the usual discomforts of late pregnancy—swollen ankles and relentless acid reflux—but is doing well. Through our regular webcam conversations, I can see that her belly has grown significantly. Modern-day technology—what a blessing!

As if on cue with the mounting anticipation, Hannah decided it was time for a "family conference." From her pink gingham-decorated room, she called us in for what she declared to be an "important discussion." With her eyes brimming with tears, she made her case: "It's not fair! You and Daddy got to name Aidan and me, so now it's my turn!" Struggling to suppress a smile, I told her that the names Rowen and Caleb had already been chosen. After we shared the heartfelt meanings behind each name, Hannah finally gave in.

December 11, 2004—this date marks a momentous chapter in our lives, pulsing with life-altering significance. Love at first sight was destined to happen twice that day, for Rowen Alexander and Caleb Monte.

Around noon, I was in the kitchen, casually assembling a salad for Kenny's annual "pizza and beer" birthday party. As I chopped and mixed, my sister kept me company over the phone, filling the air with chatter. Suddenly, call waiting buzzed in, displaying Maureen's name on the screen. Anticipation and anxiety gripped my heart. "Aarin, I have to take this," I hastily told my sister and switched lines.

"Hi, I'm at the hospital," Maureen said calmly. "I'm four centimeters dilated."

Taking a deep breath, I managed to say, "We're on our way, Maureen. Keep those babies inside you until we get there."

"Don't worry, they're not making their debut until you're here," she assured me. "But do hurry."

Switching back to Aarin, my voice tinged with excitement and panic, I blurted out, "You need to come over right now. Maureen is in labor. Cancel the party. This is happening."

The universe has a flair for timing. Just the night before, Kenny and I had penned our "Holy Shit—Hurry Up & Get Out Of The House Fast List," sparing us from thinking too much in a moment heavy with emotion.

Meanwhile, Kenny and Hannah were engrossed in *The Incredibles* at the movie theater. I dialed his number, and he picked up almost immediately. "We need to leave, Hannah," Kenny whispered to her after hanging up. "Your brothers are coming."

Kenny felt regretful for making Hannah leave the movie in the middle but was touched by her understanding. When they walked through the front door, they found me in a whirlwind of preparation, my expression a blend of urgency and unyielding determination. The kitchen table had been converted into a makeshift command center, its surface awash with papers, passports, and that handwritten checklist with lines aggressively crossed off one by one.

Neatly stacked beside the table was an array of essentials for the babies: car seats, a collapsible double stroller, blankets, and clothes—all ready for immediate use. Flights had been booked, bags were packed, and a taxi was on standby, all in anticipation of the looming snowstorm that could throw a wrench into our plans. Kenny and I shared a tender moment with Hannah and Aidan, kissing them goodbye and whispering promises of the exciting introduction to their new brothers upon our return. With a final affectionate glance, we entrusted them to Aarin's capable hands, feeling the mingled pangs of parting and the intense eagerness for the life-changing event that was just on the horizon.

"I hope this snow holds off," I muttered as the taxi pulled away, the first flakes beginning to fall. We had no time to lose.

When we reached the airport, everything unfolded as if predestined. We raced through check-in, security, and customs, boarding just in time. By 5 p.m., we had arrived in Harrisburg and made our way to the hospital. There, Maureen was a vision of calm anticipation, comfortably positioned with her epidural already administered. Jeff sat casually nearby, a quiet figure of support.

Once she reached the ten-centimeter dilation mark, because this was a twin birth, it was time to move to the operating room. Kenny and I put on sterile gowns and masks, about to witness our sons enter the world. Kenny held my hand, squeezing it ever so slightly, a silent pact between us.

At 8:30 p.m. Rowen (Baby B) was born first, slipping into the world as if guided by invisible hands. The doctor lifted him, and he let out a strong, defiant cry—the most beautiful sound. The neonatologist, a specialist in newborn intensive care, gave Rowen a quick check; he was perfectly fine and required no extra attention. My eyes locked onto his miniature frame, and a sense of déjà vu washed over me: he was a mirror image of Aidan as a newborn.

While awaiting his brother's arrival, the nurse tenderly placed Rowen into the curve of my arm. Behind me, Kenny's embrace enveloped us both, adding warmth and strength to this intimate moment. Rowen's delicate skin was satin-like, and each of his soft cries seemed to carry a whisper of new beginnings. My fingertips mapped the landscape of his tiny palms and minuscule fingernails, as if engraving each detail into my memory. Profound gratitude overwhelmed me, and tears began to trace their way down my cheeks. I whispered words of love into his tender ears, welcoming him into the world that was now infinitely better with him in it.

As we waited for Caleb (Baby A) to be born, my attention ricocheted between two pivotal scenes. One second I was beside Rowen, watching in awe as he was measured and weighed, and the next I was back at Maureen's side, encouraging her through each arduous push. The medley of beeping monitors melded with the poignant visuals: Rowen in one corner, Caleb's head beginning to crown in another. It was a tantalizing preview of what was about to become our new normal.

After thirty minutes, at 9:00 p.m., Caleb's entrance into this world was a bit more dramatic; his heart rate dipped for a brief hold-your-breath moment. As the medical team attended to him, I found myself in a strange limbo—elated yet anxious, my eyes darting from Caleb to the monitors and back again. Fortunately, his heart found its rhythm, and he would be taken to the NICU more as a precautionary measure than an immediate necessity. Before the nurses whisked him away, they placed him in my arms. In that moment, I felt a sense of contentment so pure it defied description. There he was—his delicate lips, his diminutive form wrapped in a soft blanket. I pressed my lips to his newborn face, whispering how much joy he had already given me in the mere minutes since his birth. My gaze then shifted to Kenny, who cradled Rowen with equal tenderness.

Maureen was doing wonderfully, and I knew that soon she and Jeff would be headed to her recovery room.

In those initial hours, the boys adapted to life outside the womb like seasoned pros. Our hospital room became an oasis of slowed time, allowing us to fully absorb the sheer magnitude of our transformed family. Nurses flowed in and out, their praises for the boys' progress affirming what we already knew: we were blessed.

Within forty-eight hours of Rowen and Caleb's birth, we were ready to leave the hospital. Maureen looked from me to the twins with a certain satisfaction, as though we were sharing in a secret accomplishment only we could understand. When our eyes met, I saw in hers relief, joy, and a sense of closure. Her time with us was nearing its end, but the impact of her role in our lives was beyond measure—she had birthed three of our four children. Tears flowed as we hugged her. "You're an angel, Maureen," I whispered, my voice cracking. "Thank you will never be enough."

Running on adrenaline and functioning on little more than snippets of sleep accumulated over the past two days, we arrived at the airport well ahead of schedule. We knew that tending to the needs of two newborns—feeding and changing them—would carve out its own unique chunk of time. Once we boarded the plane, Kenny and I each held a baby close to our chests, providing them warmth and security during the flight. Just like Aidan's flight home, astonishingly, they slept through the entire trip. Who could believe they'd be such peaceful travelers? As we flew back to Toronto, a surreal atmosphere surrounded us in the cabin. I couldn't wait to get home. It felt like we were floating between two realms: the life we had left behind and the life we hadn't yet come to know.

My father-in-law, Morrey, greeted us at the airport, his presence a soothing contrast to the bustling days we had just experienced. When he first saw his grandsons, his eyes sparkled with emotion, and a smile stretched from cheek to cheek. He pulled Kenny into a heartfelt embrace, a gesture rich with the love and pride of a father and grandfather meeting the newest additions to the family.

As we approached our driveway, my heartbeat quickened in anticipation. When the front door swung open, there stood Hannah and Aidan, their faces practically luminous with uncontainable excitement.

"You're finally home!" Hannah exclaimed.

My mother-in-law, Lenore, was also there, her eyes shining with happiness as she took in the tender scene. And then the moment arrived, sitting on the couch, we gently laid Rowen into Hannah's prepared arms and Caleb into Aidan's. Despite his tender age of not quite two years, Aidan cradled Caleb with an uncanny sense of the moment's weight. Hannah, her face radiant with a newfound sisterly pride, held Rowen as if he were the most cherished gift.

We then orchestrated a switch—Hannah now holding Caleb, Aidan taking Rowen—and the air filled with an almost magical sense of unity and possibility. The room hummed with an extraordinary new energy. It was as if we were all being initiated into a richer, fuller life, replete with the promise of shared experiences, challenges, and unconditional love. The array of baby bottles, sleepless nights, and first steps lay ahead, but in that moment, it felt as if the universe had aligned just for us.

"Ready for the adventure of our lives?" Kenny asked, grinning.

"Bring it on," I replied, each syllable infused with eagerness for the roller-coaster ride we had just embarked upon.

Dearest Reader: When have you encountered a moment where you felt a profound sense of transformation and closure?

MILE 23

LIFE AFTER SURROGACY

Once Aidan arrived, it was as if the core of my being had pivoted. The void that once felt insatiable began to close; not completely, but enough to breathe easier. I still mourned my inability to bear more children, but the urgency that once consumed me had softened. *Have you ever felt suspended in time—aware that you're at a standstill even as the world spins on, milestones coming and going, life unspooling regardless of the invisible tethers holding you back?*

When Rowen and Caleb joined our family, it's not that I didn't reflect on the rugged path that led us there; it's more that the day-to-day reality of raising four children left little room for rumination. Or perhaps I'd endured enough heartache to last a lifetime and had no wish to reopen old wounds. Or maybe—just maybe—I had found a peace that eluded definition. I had the family I'd always yearned for, and that was enough to keep me rooted in the present, eager for whatever would come next.

<u>September 6, 2007</u>

My dear journal, it's hard to believe that more than three years have slipped by since I last confided in your pages. Today, something—perhaps the tug of nostalgia—compelled me to seek you out. My story, it seems, yearns for a fitting epilogue.

Our house is now a hubbub of laughter, curiosity, and, yes, the occasional sibling squabble.

Hannah, now eight, possesses a memory that never ceases to amaze. After listening to Alison's Zinnia by Anita Lobel just once, she could recite every flower corresponding to each letter of the alphabet.

And then there's four-year-old Aidan, our little social ambassador. On his first day of junior kindergarten, he went from one child to another, inviting each one to play. By the end of the day, he'd turned a roomful of strangers into a circle of friends.

Rowen and Caleb are two-and-a-half-year-old bundles of surprise. While Rowen climbs bookshelves and gives me mini heart attacks, Caleb sits amid his building blocks, almost as if he's deciphering the physics behind them.

Their imaginations blend beautifully in the make-believe restaurant they've set up in our basement. Under Hannah's directive eye, roles are swiftly assigned. She's the uncompromising chef, Aidan the welcoming host, Rowen the hustling server, and Caleb the ever-observant patron.

This inventive world they've crafted isn't just child's play; it's a microcosm of their burgeoning personalities and the genuine bonds they share. They laugh, argue, play, and love; and Kenny and I get to be the lucky spectators of these priceless moments.

In 1999, if someone had leaned in and whispered a prophecy of me becoming a mother to four remarkable children—after a doctor had painted a bleak picture of future motherhood—I might have dismissed it as mere fantasy. Yet, having ridden this tumultuous rollercoaster of hope, heartbreak, and eventual triumph, I've come to see each unexpected bend as a manifestation of grace.

Today, I am more than just a mom; I mentor others wading through the complex waters of alternative paths to parenthood. With each piece of advice I give, I find a piece of the mentor I wish I had had years ago.

As if to seal this chapter of our lives, we'll share our story on national TV tomorrow. It feels like the universe's way of saying, "Your tale is worth telling." A public affirmation of the enduring power of love, resilience, strength, and the varied journeys toward building a family.

And so, as this season comes to an end, another inevitably begins. What awaits us is unknown, and yet I am ready; we are ready—forever buoyed by the love that has brought us this far.

Once I had set my sights on conquering the NYC Marathon, the fire of my unwavering determination took over—much like it did on my path toward expanding our family. In both scenarios, my tenacity (or, as some might call it, stubbornness) propelled me forward. As I reflect on our surrogacy journey, it felt as though I was leading two parallel lives, each with its unique rhythm: one was a high-speed vortex celebrating Hannah's growth and milestones, and the other was a slow-motion obstacle course filled with challenges on the road to having another child.

After Aidan's birth, I felt an innate sense of responsibility to help other couples maneuver through the complexities of surrogacy. I started receiving calls from women who had heard about our experience from various sources—family, friends, our fertility lawyers, and even through local community chatter. The knowledge I had gathered over those challenging years morphed into more than just individual insight; it became a valuable resource I could offer to others on this demanding journey. Each time I received the wonderful news that a surrogate for a couple I'd guided was pregnant, I was overcome with emotion. Invitations to their baby showers and family gatherings were more than just social events; they were affirmations of the small yet appreciated role I'd played in bringing new life into the world.

This work didn't just instill a sense of pride; it offered me a deep understanding of my own experiences. Confronting fertility issues is a formidable challenge, but the realization that I could alleviate some of that weight for others filled me with an unmistakable sense of purpose.

From the time our boys could understand the concept of birth, we recounted their unique story, emphasizing that they grew in our hearts, not in my womb. We wanted them to grasp the immensity of our love for them, even before their conception.

We also revealed another remarkable aspect of their story. Though our three boys arrived in this world at different times, they have a bond even rarer than that of typical siblings—they are biologically triplets. Created from the same batch of embryos, their shared origin serves as evidence of the intricate wonders of life and science. Strangely enough, the universe seemed to foreshadow their arrival when the car with the "TRIPLETS" licence plate passed us, just before Maureen revealed she was pregnant with Aidan. They are a trio, not bound by simultaneous birth but by a common starting point that makes their connection all the more meaningful.

The balancing act of parenthood, especially with four young children, has been exhilarating yet precarious, with many quivering steps and unsteady moments. Initially, the task felt Herculean, but what began as my life's greatest challenge has transformed into its most rewarding adventure. I have not just watched my children grow; I have grown with them.

I am utterly amazed at how quickly they have blossomed into adulthood. Hannah is now twenty-five, Aidan is twenty-one, and Rowen and Caleb are twenty. Our home, once a whirlwind of laughter, youthful energy, and the purest love, has evolved. The days when the air was filled with the tunes from *Thomas the Train* and *The Wiggles*, when the garden was a playground of sprinklers and sandboxes, and when bedtime stories were the grand finale to our daily escapades—those days are etched in my memory. They're both a sweet remembrance and a poignant reminder of the relentless march of time. It's a sentiment that resonates with any parent who has watched their children outgrow childhood right before their eyes.

Every tear wiped, every scraped knee bandaged, every moral lesson imparted—it's all been a two-way street. I've learned as much from them as they've learned from me: the art of patience, the strength of unconditional love, and the profound joy that comes from watching someone you've nurtured find their own footing in the world.

When Rowen and Caleb were just two years old, I was at a crossroads. I had to go back to work, but the idea of resuming my vocation in environmental management meant I'd miss out on my children's formative years. Fitness had been a long-standing passion of mine, and it offered the work-life balance I was searching for. After earning certifications in spin instruction and personal training, I embarked on a new career path. For the first seven years, I dedicated myself to teaching various strength training classes at a local athletic facility. Then, seeking to diversify my experience, I transitioned to teaching spin classes at a nearby cycle studio. Simultaneously, I launched my personal training business from my home gym. This progression in my career not only allowed me to immerse myself in multiple aspects of fitness, aligning with my growing expertise, but it also enabled me to blend my professional life with my commitment to family. This harmony was crucial, allowing me to be fully present during my children's upbringing.

The COVID-19 pandemic changed the game. Gyms shuttered, but the need for physical wellness remained. That's when I started teaching free workouts on Instagram Live. What began as a community service turned into a business venture, ABS Fitness, an online fitness platform, co-founded with Kenny. Today, I balance my time between my home studio and our expanding online platform.

HHT remains an open chapter, a perpetual undercurrent in my life's story. Regular check-ups with Dr. Faughnan at

St. Michael's Hospital are a routine part of my existence, embraced with acceptance. While aware of the possibilities, I refuse to worry about the unknowns.

Kenny is the anchor of our family, consistently showing his love through actions that matter. His role as a father is truly exceptional, marked by his patience and an attentive ear that ensures our children always feel heard, valued, and understood. His approach to parenting blends gentle guidance with enthusiastic involvement. He celebrates the uniqueness of each child, acknowledging and nurturing their distinct strengths and interests, which has helped them to cultivate a grounded sense of confidence to pursue their ambitions. The depth of Kenny's impact as a father is both profound and lasting, shaping our children's lives with love, wisdom, and encouragement.

Outdoors, he's at his best, fully engaged, whether he's hiking or biking. Technology also captivates him; he's always exploring the latest gadgets and software. Professionally, he is celebrated for his talent in empowering leaders and their teams, fostering enhanced job performance across the board. Rather than merely fulfilling obligations, he possesses an innate ability to enable organizations and their employees to consistently surpass expectations and realize their fullest capabilities. The impact Kenny has is multifaceted. In our family, he's a reliable and loving presence. In his outdoor pursuits, he serves as an example of how to engage fully with the world around us. In tech, he's a continuous learner. And in his career, he's a catalyst for growth and confidence. He's not just passing through these different aspects of life; he's leaving a lasting, positive imprint.

Hannah has recently earned her Master of Science in marine biology from Dalhousie University in Halifax, Nova Scotia. Her groundbreaking thesis explored the intersections between whale habitats and human activity across the Atlantic Ocean. This included vessel and fishing activity, as well as the impact of climate change on these encounters. On top of that, she's written her own book, aimed to help nonscientists understand climate change and what they can do to mitigate its effects. *A Guide to Going Green* is available on Amazon.

When she isn't deep into her research, she spends her time working with various ocean-focused nonprofits that help facilitate the uptake of marine biology in school curriculums across the globe, rescue injured or distressed marine animals, encourage gender equity within science, and protect and clean the Canadian Atlantic Ocean and coastline.

Hannah's vibrant personality and eclectic interests add a unique dimension to her professional pursuits, infusing her scientific work with originality and innovation. Her ability to weave her appreciation for vintage aesthetics into her everyday life not only showcases her eye for detail but also reflects her approach to sustainable living. This blend of style and substance makes her stand out in any setting, inspiring those around her with her passion and commitment to making a difference. Her caring and approachable nature enhance her effectiveness in collaboration and leadership.

I admire her creativity and the importance she places on authenticity. In many ways, I see a reflection of myself in her, especially in her persistent determination and tenacity. She fully embraces her individuality and doesn't compromise her beliefs or principles.

Life After Surrogacy

Navigating his fourth year at McGill University in Montreal, Aidan has delved deep into his major in urban studies, a field that seems to echo his own intricate blueprint of empathy, intelligence, and compassion. When he speaks, it's not just words but his character that resonates—acting like a compass that directs not just him but also those lucky enough to be in his orbit. It's hard to miss the earnestness in his voice, the analytical rigor in his arguments, and the authentic love that seems to fuel his perspectives on social inclusion and life. With Aidan, lessons on embracing diversity and living authentically aren't mere conversations; they are lived experiences that he generously shares, making us all a little wiser, braver, and better.

His appreciation for music is both expansive and discerning, covering a spectrum that includes the poetic artistry of Joni Mitchell, the lyrically vivid songs of John Denver, and the soulful compositions of Ryan Beatty. Aidan is also an extraordinarily talented photographer. Through his lens, he has an uncanny ability to capture the essence of a place, each photograph serving as a vibrant snapshot that testifies to his keen eye for detail and composition.

Aidan's resilience isn't solely rooted in his character and values; it's also shaped by his life-altering diagnosis of Type 1 Diabetes (T1D) in February 2019. Seemingly benign symptoms—a thirst that water couldn't quench and frequent visits to the restroom—soon swelled into a harsh reality that shifted the axis of our family life and his forever.

The guilt gnaws at me still. I had dismissed his thirst as seasonal, overlooked the frequency of his bathroom trips, and, most hauntingly, failed to recognize the subtle weight loss hidden beneath his baggy clothing. Holding his delicate frame in that hospital bed, a tidal wave of regret hit me. Anger toward myself surged: *How could I have missed these signs when I prided myself on parental vigilance?* While logic tells me it's not my fault that he has T1D, the struggle to absolve myself continues.

Aidan refused to let his diagnosis confine or define him. Right from the start, he took it upon himself to understand every nuance of managing T1D. He became proficient in monitoring his blood glucose levels, knowledgeable about the ins and outs of insulin administration, and adept at utilizing the technical equipment that aids in his daily management. His unyielding dedication to managing his condition marks him as a true warrior.

Whether exploring foreign lands or delighting in global culinary adventures, he remains unbounded. This condition didn't diminish him; instead, it added another layer to his already rich spirit. Almost six years have passed since that gut-wrenching day, and Aidan's indomitable will to thrive, irrespective of his condition, isn't just remarkable—it's a living, breathing inspiration to us all.

Rowen is in his third year at Queens University in Kingston, Ontario, with media studies as his major. His courage, a trait so vividly etched into his character, is impossible to overlook.

Years ago, when the boys were in the playground, an older, much bigger child began to bully Aidan. Without hesitation, Rowen—then all of five years old and half the size—marched up to the bully and defended his older brother, declaring, "Don't talk to my brother that way. Leave him alone." His bravery and steadfast dedication to standing up for what was right wasn't staged; it emanated naturally.

Life After Surrogacy

Rowen is not one to merely observe life from the sidelines. Much like a Pittsburgh Steelers defensive lineman—his favorite team, and a nod to his Pennsylvania birth—he tackles challenges head-on, always aiming for a game-changing impact. His determination is especially evident from the time, at age nine, he missed the cut for the select hockey team—a team that represents a higher level of competition in the sport. He worked tirelessly to improve his game, and the following season he made the Single-A team (a level higher than select), proving his resilience and commitment to growth. He's naturally inquisitive, delving into experiences not outlined in any syllabus. You could almost say he's "minoring in curiosity," with a focus on unscripted life opportunities. When Rowen isn't excelling on the ice in hockey or making impressive plays on the basketball court, he's flashing that infectious smile—a magnetic force of good that's as genuine as it is contagious.

Caleb may be the youngest of his siblings, but he stands tallest—both in stature and in quiet influence. Also in his third year at Queens University, he's diving into economics, a field that mirrors his analytical bent. Don't let his reserved demeanor fool you; he's always attuned to his surroundings, picking up details many might overlook.

Rather than speaking out to fill the silence, Caleb opts to let his actions take the lead. In the summer of 2020, during the COVID-19 pandemic, he showcased this trait in an extraordinary way: he rallied Rowen and a group of four friends to run 124 miles (200 km) over the course of four days from Toronto to Haliburton, Ontario, raising over $40,000 for The Terry Fox Foundation. A few years ago, he also captained his hockey team, leading them to the City

Championships. He's not just committed to sharpening his mind; he's equally devoted to physical excellence and rigorously maintains his athleticism.

Caleb embodies a rare combination of emotional vulnerability and resilience. When he's moved or inspired, it shows, and that humble openness only deepens the respect others have for him. When Caleb sets his sights on a goal, he approaches it with an unstoppable determination.

In the mosaic of our family's life, each person—Hannah, Aidan, Rowen, Caleb, Kenny, and myself—serves as a distinct and vital piece, united by love and a mutual commitment. From the individual triumphs and trials to our shared experiences, every moment has enriched my life. And while my children continue to shape their own futures, I realize that my role in guiding them is far from finished. It remains my life's most rewarding pursuit. What a privilege it is to travel this infinite path of growth beside them.

A reflection of this unity was our trip to New York City for the marathon. My mom, Kenny, Hannah, and Aidan came with me. Adam, his wife, Lindsey, and their kids, Rylee and Hudson, joined as well, and Aarin brought her daughter, Dylan. We had strong family support all around. My father, increasingly anxious about travel in his later years, was upset that he couldn't attend in person. Instead, he stayed home, watching the race intently on his iPad, tracking our every move from start to finish with the NYC Marathon app. Rowen and Caleb, busy with school and midterms, were unable to come along, but I felt their presence and encouragement from afar. I'll never forget reaching the 25-mile (40.2 km) mark and hearing Aidan shout, "Mom, Alison!" as he stood perched up high on a lamppost. He'd managed to raise his voice over the roar of the rest of the crowd, just enough to capture my attention. And there they were—my family, cheering from the sidelines and reminding me, *Just one more mile to go, you've got this.*

Dearest Reader: How have the challenges and joys in your life shaped you?

MILE 24

LESSONS LEARNED

Life encompasses laughter and sorrow, sometimes intertwined and sometimes separate. It presents us with constant opportunities, cleverly disguised as setbacks or failures. This duality is laid out before us, urging acknowledgment. It manifests in our presence, our adaptability, our ability to pivot, and our strides toward progress.

Upon revisiting the pages of my journals for this book, I felt a surge of pride. How often do we genuinely take the time to reflect on past events and recognize, appreciate, and celebrate our strength, courage, and personal growth? Running a marathon taught me invaluable lessons in perseverance, yet I failed to realize that I had already possessed an underlying foundation of inner resilience. I had navigated marathons before, not in the literal or physical sense, but in an emotional and mental capacity. And I believe we all have.

During our surrogacy journey, each setback felt like a crushing blow. I remember gripping the phone as the voice on the other end softly uttered, "It didn't take," and feeling my heart plummet. The injections, those sharp cold needles that seemed like daily betrayals, each one a prick of hope and doubt. And the appointments—oh, the countless doctor's visits where we would sit waiting in clinical rooms, flipping through outdated magazines, my eyes meeting Kenny's in a silent exchange of optimism and dread. Each night, as I lay in bed, I found myself whispering prayers into the silence, praying to a God who seemed more abstract with each passing day. "Please, if you're there, help us," I would beg, not knowing if my words were even heard. In those moments, my prayers felt less like a calling to the divine and more like an existential dialogue with myself.

Surrogacy turned my life inside out, as if shaking a snow globe and watching each flake find its new resting place. I see now the lessons hidden within those years of trying. I was focused on the destination, blind to the scenery along the way. During that period, I felt like a boat stuck in a storm, longing for the safety of the harbor. But here's what I didn't realize: the storm itself had lessons to teach me—lessons about patience, surrender, and the intricate interplay of human emotions. Amid these trials, Hannah's very presence compelled me to muster the strength required to conquer this intensely challenging chapter of my life. Her unfiltered innocence endowed me with a fortitude I hadn't known before. For almost four years, I felt like I was holding my breath, and it took me that long to understand that I could still find air, even in the suffocating weight of waiting.

I've discovered that resilience is akin to a muscle that requires consistent exercise and nurturing. Like physical strength, resilience grows stronger when faced with challenges and adversity. It is through resilience that we find the strength to persevere and overcome obstacles, building our capacity to endure the complexities of life.

I've come to understand that failure is not a definitive endpoint but rather a gateway to new opportunities. Instead of viewing failure as a negative outcome, I now embrace it as a valuable teacher. It is through our failures that we learn, grow, and discover alternative paths that lead us toward success. Each setback presents a chance to reassess, adapt, and approach our goals with renewed determination.

I've learned the importance of granting ourselves the gift of grace. It is easy to be self-critical and harsh in times of difficulty or when we make mistakes. However, extending compassion and forgiveness to ourselves is essential for personal growth and healing. By embracing grace, we create a nurturing environment that allows us to learn from our experiences, cultivate self-acceptance, and move forward with resilience.

Throughout my life, I've discovered the crucial role that gut instincts play in shaping our decisions. These inner promptings, while sometimes subtle and hard to put into words, are vital in our decision-making process. We should balance intuition with thoughtful consideration, acknowledging its voice and reflecting on it. Our intuition can act like an inner adviser, providing insights and perspectives, particularly in times of uncertainty or ambiguity.

In light of all I've experienced, one pivotal lesson emerges with unmistakable clarity: the importance of self-advocacy. In the past, I'd let medical professionals guide me unquestioningly, a deference that cost me both emotionally and physically.

Over time, I came to appreciate the power and necessity of questions. They became my tool for probing deeper, for challenging the status quo, and for aligning external advice with my internal compass. Far from a sign of mistrust or confrontation, asking questions became an act of partnership and engagement in my own well-being.

I started to exercise my voice in various areas of my life, refusing to let anyone else's judgment silence my own. No longer would I let a title, an office, or the appearance of expertise deter me from pursuing what felt right for me. I learned to place a high value on my intuition, using it as a barometer for decision-making.

The transition from passive participant to engaged advocate is substantial, with profound implications. It's not just about speaking up; it's about actively empowering yourself to shape your destiny, realizing that your voice, questions, and challenges are valid and essential. This insight into the power of self-advocacy didn't just change how I approach healthcare—it reshaped how I engage with the world.

Looking back, I see that resilience, self-advocacy, understanding failure, and intuitive discernment aren't isolated lessons; they're interconnected, each enriching the others within the ecosystem of personal growth. One gave me the courage to practice the other. For instance, the more I advocated for myself, the more resilient I became. The stronger my resilience, the better I handled failures, turning them into opportunities for progress. I used to measure my life by big milestones: buying a house, expanding our family, running a marathon. But now I see that the smaller steps in between are just as important. Those "in-between" moments, sometimes guided by instinctive insight, are the driving force behind my perseverance. They're the building blocks that make up the bigger picture of my life, and they

...erve celebration too. The value isn't solely in reaching the endpoint; it's in savoring each nuanced segment of the path.

Dearest Reader: What challenges in your own life have served as hidden opportunities for growth and self-advocacy?

MILE 25

RACE DAY

Life unfolds in a way that defies prediction, a mysterious blend of planned events and unforeseen twists. We set objectives—*but why? What drives us to break past the boundaries of what we thought we could accomplish?*

For me, the marathon epitomized this quest. Covering 26.2 miles in 4 hours, 54 minutes, and 6 seconds was like conquering an internal Everest—a feat of mental endurance more than anything else.

My insomnia was my companion on the eve of the race. I lay awake, assaulted by a cacophony of what-ifs and minutiae—everything from the unpredictability of the weather to the availability of functional portable toilets. By 4:30 a.m., my mind was racing more quickly than I had hoped, so I rose, the rush of energy masking my sleep deprivation.

A sip of coffee, a nibble on a banana. My stomach churned in rhythm with my thoughts. I geared up, donned my running shoes, and locked eyes with my reflection in the mirror. Then I woke up my family—Kenny, Hannah, and Aidan—for final hugs. Their touch and encouraging words stayed with me as I stepped out of the room.

In the hotel lobby, I met my sister. Together, we hailed a taxi to the 7 a.m. Midtown ferry. The city was still enveloped in pre-dawn quietude, the sky a canvas for the rising sun's brushstrokes of pink and orange—hues of unfolding promise.

Arriving on Staten Island, we joined my brother. A shared sense of purpose united us amid the chaotic backdrop of tens of thousands of other runners. With different start times, Adam set off first, followed by Aarin and then me. Saying our goodbyes at the corrals, I was overwhelmed by emotion.

The starting line buzzed with an electricity that was almost tactile. I could smell the asphalt beneath us mingling with the nervous perspiration of nearby runners. It was as if the pavement itself was going to join us, a living entity that swelled and ebbed with our collective breath. We each seemed lost in contemplation, pondering the miles that lay ahead.

Fueled by adrenaline, I covered the first six miles at a pace unsustainable for my stamina. Inescapable humidity filled the air, as sweat trickled down my forehead. My pulse hammered in my ears, a drumroll of caution for my overzealous start. Now, it was a mental game on a physical battlefield. I slowed down, hydrating at each water station, consuming energy chews and Gatorade, and attuning to my body's signals.

Midway, something within me shifted. A newfound conviction eclipsed earlier anxieties. Running through the city's vibrant boroughs, the crowd's roars became a distant melody that underscored my internal dialogue.

The final miles were arduous. My skin sticky with the sheen of effort, I could taste the salt on my lips. With just a mile left, I spotted Kenny reaching out his hand. Clenching it for a fleeting second, a lump formed in my throat—emotion, raw and unfiltered. I saw Hannah and Aidan and my mom cheering. "I can do hard things," I whispered to myself.

Race Day

Each step through Central Park was a push-pull of exhilaration and exhaustion. Approaching the finish, a wave of euphoria washed over me. One step at a time, I crossed that line.

The moment was an emotional kaleidoscope—happiness, exhaustion, awe, pain, and a towering sense of personal pride. So absorbed was I in the feelings that I barely registered the volunteer placing the medal around my neck. It wasn't just a symbol; it came to represent a part of who I am.

As I stood there, the cool medal contrasting against my flushed skin, a revelation crystallized within me. I had embarked on this marathon believing it would teach me about perseverance, resilience, and inner strength. But in that moment, I understood that the marathon didn't instill these qualities in me; it revealed what had been there all along. It was not a transformation but an affirmation. I didn't just discover my ability to persevere; I realized it had carried me every step of the way.

Back at the hotel, reuniting with Adam and Aarin brought a wave of fulfillment, a testament to our collective achievement. In their faces, I saw the day's weariness etched in lines that hadn't been there in our youth, yet their eyes sparkled with the same elation we had as kids after a day of adventurous play. This juxtaposition of past and present, of the children we once were and the adults we've become, was a poignant reminder of our shared journey through life.

Celebrating in a cozy Chinese restaurant, the gleam of our medals mingled with the ambient light. We reminisced about the race, each story revealing a unique struggle and an opportunity to persevere. Adam's face, flushed from the day's humidity, showed the toll of him pushing his limits, his resolve tested but intact. As the evening unfolded, he met with a funny predicament: his legs, completely depleted, were no match for the formidable stairs leading down to the restaurant bathroom. With humor and pragmatism, he decided to forgo the precarious descent and wait it out, another test of his resolve, so to speak. Aarin recounted with a mischievous smile her "audacious" choice to consume Gatorade early in the marathon, veering from her standard training regimen. This gamble, taken against the time-honored advice of not trying anything new on race day, weighed on her for much of the course. As she progressed, the specter of potential "runs of the non-running variety" loomed large, one that, thankfully, never became a reality.

As life moves forward, every Saturday morning, the three of us continue to meet for our regular 6.2-mile (10 km) run. In these moments, I'm reminded of how fortunate I am to have Adam and Aarin in my life. These runs are far more than a physical exercise; they're a manifestation of the incredible bond we share as siblings, a connection that continues to thrive beyond the confines of any race.

Dearest Reader: What internal strength and resilience lie within you?

MILE 26.2

HOPE

Hope isn't merely a transient feeling; it's a deliberate, brave decision—a constant ally that held my hand through surrogacy, the maze of fertility treatments, and the intricacies of connecting with gestational carriers. It was my resilience in the face of disappointments and my enlightenment through unexpected revelations. This hope was not an abstract concept; it was as tangible as the sweat and determination of my marathon, each stride echoing a small victory in self-discovery.

This hope manifested itself in subtle yet significant ways. It was not in overt gestures but in the quiet, heart-wrenching exchanges of empathy with fellow women at the fertility clinics. Each glance spoke volumes, conveying a mutual understanding—a common recognition of shared struggles and a yearning so intense that we would go to the ends of the earth to fulfill it. It was in the cheers of bystanders during the marathon; their support acted as a crucial reinforcement that fortified my inner strength, reminding me that I was part of something greater, even in moments of isolation or despair.

As we navigate the marathon of life, our focus often shifts according to conventional milestones. In youth, we may long for the freedoms and opportunities that adulthood promises. During our twenties, the chase often involves careers and new experiences. The thirties can usher in the complexity of family dynamics, and by the time we reach our forties, we may find ourselves deeply entrenched in responsibilities. Yet, regardless of age, many of us reach a midlife reckoning—a universal pause, if you will—where we assess our achievements, reconsider our values, and recalibrate our aspirations.

As I find myself now on the other side of these life-altering milestones, the haunting question that once consumed me—*Why me?*—has undergone a radical transformation. What was once a cry for explanation is now a whisper of profound gratitude. The answer, I realize, doesn't need to be explicitly defined; it echoes in the laughter of my children, the unconditional love of my husband, and the incomparable joy of crossing hard-fought finish lines. This new *Why me?* is no longer a burden to bear but a celebration of the blessings I've worked so hard to attain. And while I'm fully aware that the road ahead may present more *Why me?* moments, the deep-rooted hope that has guided me so far reassures me that I'll have the strength to face, and perhaps even welcome, the miles I have yet to run.

Dearest Reader: Where does your hope live?

MILE 27

TBD

An open road awaits…

ACKNOWLEDGMENTS

Writing this memoir has been as challenging, rewarding, and transformative as running my actual marathon. In 1999, my journal pages became the canvas for my intensely personal journey into surrogacy. I dreamed these writings would one day serve as a legacy to my future children, illustrating that they were born from profound love and commitment—a heart that yearned to bear them, paired with a body that couldn't.

Closing that third journal signified both an ending and a new beginning. As the ink dried on its pages, I felt a deep intuition that these experiences would someday form the foundation of this book. When my four incredible children began their university studies, I found myself with newfound time and space. This liberty propelled me through two distinct yet intertwined marathons: one with running shoes on, pounding the pavement of physical endurance, and another behind a keyboard, wrestling with words and emotions.

To our surrogate M., thank you for your unbridled dedication in helping us bring our three sons into the world. Words of gratitude will never be enough.

To my four children, Hannah, Aidan, Rowen, and Caleb. The blessings that you have brought to my life are boundless. Thank you for filling my heart with love, learning, and immeasurable joy. You can achieve anything you work hard for; and when you fail, stand up, dust yourself off, and surge forward. You are all living proof that persistence enables you to prevail.

To Kenny. I love you. I love you because you traveled this road with me. I love you because you helped show me that vulnerability is strength. I love you because you held me up through all the trials and tribulations of our surrogacy journey. I love you because together we brought four wonderful human beings into the world. I love you for always biking alongside me and for being my greatest cheerleader. I love you for loving me.

To my mother, Sharron, your unwavering love, strength, and support have been the constants in my life. It was you who cheered the loudest and cried the hardest as I crossed the finish line in New York.

To my father, Robert, you nurtured my love for running, taught me humility, and instilled a belief that I could overcome any obstacle. You showed me how to be my own hero.

To my brother, Adam, and my sister, Aarin, my trusted running companions. Your constant love, generosity, and support have been cornerstones in my life.

To our extended families and friends, your love and understanding have been indispensable.

To the doctors, nurses, lawyers, fertility specialists, and social workers, your expertise and kindness helped make our dream a reality.

To Ellyn Franklin, whose guidance was instrumental in transforming my journals into a compelling narrative, providing me with a crucial outline to craft this engaging memoir.

Acknowledgments

To Heather Sangster, thank you for your exceptional editorial support in fine-tuning this manuscript. Your insights and guidance have been invaluable.

To Jordan Lunn, thank you for your collaboration on the cover design. Your constant support and willingness to make even the smallest changes have been greatly appreciated.

To Kenny, Hannah, and Aidan, whose critical insights illuminated what was missing and showed me how to tell my story more effectively. To my grandmother Pearl, whose early reading of my manuscript provided me with steadfast faith and insistence that everything would fall into place. And to my dad, your discerning insights and meticulous corrections were very helpful.

To Judy L. and Tamara S., who generously devoted their time to pore over my initial manuscript and offered heartfelt and constructive feedback. And to Dr. Faughnan, for taking the time to read through my chapter on HHT, ensuring that I accurately summarized this disease.

To my proofreaders, ARC (Advance Reading Copy) readers, and everyone else who provided feedback and insight—I am deeply grateful for your contributions. Thank you.